CONTENTS

1. Guess the Number Game

```
#include <iostream>
#include <cstdlib>
#include <ctime>
using namespace std;
int main() {
    srand(time(0)); // Seed the random number generator
    int secretNumber = rand() % 100 + 1; // Generate random number between 1 and 100
    int guess;
    int attempts = 0;
    cout << "Welcome to Guess the Number game!\n";
    cout << "I have selected a number between 1 and 100. Try to guess it.\n\n";
    do {
        cout << "Enter your guess: ";
        cin >> guess;
        attempts++;
        if (guess > secretNumber) {
            cout << "Too high! Try again.\n";
        } else if (guess < secretNumber) {
            cout << "Too low! Try again.\n";
        } else {
            cout << "Congratulations! You've guessed the correct number in " << attempts << "
attempts!\n";
        }
    } while (guess != secretNumber);
    return 0;
}
```

This program generates a random number between 1 and 100 and asks the user to guess the number. It provides feedback whether the guess is too high or too low and continues until the correct number is guessed. Finally, it displays the number of attempts taken to guess the correct number.

2. Rock, Paper, Scissors

```
#include <iostream>
#include <cstdlib>
#include <ctime>
using namespace std;
// Function to get computer's choice
string computerChoice() {
    int randomNum = rand() % 3;
    if (randomNum == 0) {
        return "Rock";
    } else if (randomNum == 1) {
        return "Paper";
    } else {
        return "Scissors";
    }
}
// Function to determine the winner
string determineWinner(string player, string computer) {
    if (player == computer) {
        return "It's a tie!";
    } else if ((player == "Rock" && computer == "Scissors") ||
            (player == "Paper" && computer == "Rock") ||
            (player == "Scissors" && computer == "Paper")) {
        return "You win!";
    } else {
        return "Computer wins!";
    }
}
int main() {
    srand(time(0)); // Seed the random number generator
    string choices[3] = {"Rock", "Paper", "Scissors"};
    string playerChoice, computerChoice;
    cout << "Welcome to Rock, Paper, Scissors!\n";
    cout << "Enter your choice (Rock, Paper, or Scissors): ";
    cin >> playerChoice;
```

```
    // Validate user input
    while (playerChoice != "Rock" && playerChoice != "Paper" && playerChoice != "Scissors") {
        cout << "Invalid choice. Please enter Rock, Paper, or Scissors: ";
        cin >> playerChoice;
    }
    // Get computer's choice
    computerChoice = computerChoice();
    cout << "You chose: " << playerChoice << endl;
    cout << "Computer chose: " << computerChoice << endl;
    // Determine the winner
    cout << determineWinner(playerChoice, computerChoice) << endl;
    return 0;
}
```

3. Dice Roll Simulator

```
#include <iostream>
#include <cstdlib>
#include <ctime>
using namespace std;
int rollDice() {
    // Generate a random number between 1 and 6
    return rand() % 6 + 1;
}
int main() {
    srand(time(0)); // Seed the random number generator
    char playAgain;
    do {
        cout << "Welcome to the Dice Roll Simulator!\n";
        cout << "You rolled: " << rollDice() << endl;
        cout << "Do you want to roll again? (Y/N): ";
        cin >> playAgain;
    } while (playAgain == 'Y' || playAgain == 'y');
    cout << "Thanks for playing!\n";
    return 0;
}
```

4. Hangman Game

```
#include <iostream>
#include <string>
#include <cstdlib>
#include <ctime>
using namespace std;
string chooseWord() {
  // Array of words to choose from
  string words[] = {"apple", "banana", "orange", "grape", "pineapple", "strawberry",
"watermelon", "kiwi"};
    // Get the number of words in the array
  int numWords = sizeof(words) / sizeof(words[0]);
    // Generate a random index
  int randomIndex = rand() % numWords;
    // Return the randomly chosen word
  return words[randomIndex];
}
bool contains(char letter, const string& word) {
  // Check if the letter is present in the word
  for (char c : word) {
    if (c == letter) {
      return true;
    }
  }
  return false;
}
void displayWord(const string& word, const string& guessedLetters) {
  // Display the word with guessed letters visible, others hidden
  for (char c : word) {
    if (guessedLetters.find(c) != string::npos) {
      cout << c << " ";
    } else {
      cout << "_ ";
    }
  }
```

```
    cout << endl;
}
int main() {
    srand(time(0)); // Seed the random number generator
    string word = chooseWord();
    string guessedLetters;
    int attemptsLeft = 6;
    cout << "Welcome to Hangman!\n";
    while (attemptsLeft > 0) {
        cout << "Word: ";
        displayWord(word, guessedLetters);
            if (word == guessedLetters) {
            cout << "Congratulations! You've guessed the word: " << word << endl;
            break;
        }
        cout << "Attempts left: " << attemptsLeft << endl;
        cout << "Guess a letter: ";
        char guess;
        cin >> guess;
        if (contains(guess, word)) {
            cout << "Correct guess!\n";
            guessedLetters += guess;
        } else {
            cout << "Incorrect guess!\n";
            attemptsLeft--;
        }
            cout << endl;
    }
        if (attemptsLeft == 0) {
        cout << "Sorry, you've run out of attempts. The word was: " << word << endl;
    }
        cout << "Thanks for playing Hangman!\n";
        return 0;
}
```

5. Tic-Tac-Toe

```
#include <iostream>
#include <vector>
#include <string>
using namespace std;
// Function to print the tic-tac-toe board
void printBoard(const vector<vector<char>>& board) {
    for (int i = 0; i < 3; ++i) {
        for (int j = 0; j < 3; ++j) {
            cout << board[i][j];
            if (j < 2) {
                cout << " | ";
            }
        }
        cout << endl;
        if (i < 2) {
            cout << "---------" << endl;
        }
    }
}
// Function to check if someone wins
char checkWinner(const vector<vector<char>>& board) {
    // Check rows
    for (int i = 0; i < 3; ++i) {
        if (board[i][0] == board[i][1] && board[i][1] == board[i][2] && board[i][0] != ' ') {
            return board[i][0];
        }
    }
    // Check columns
    for (int i = 0; i < 3; ++i) {
        if (board[0][i] == board[1][i] && board[1][i] == board[2][i] && board[0][i] != ' ') {
            return board[0][i];
        }
    }
```

```
    // Check diagonals
    if (board[0][0] == board[1][1] && board[1][1] == board[2][2] && board[0][0] != ' ') {
        return board[0][0];
    }
    if (board[0][2] == board[1][1] && board[1][1] == board[2][0] && board[0][2] != ' ') {
        return board[0][2];
    }
    return ' '; // If no winner yet
}
int main() {
    vector<vector<char>> board(3, vector<char>(3, ' ')); // Initialize empty board
    bool player1Turn = true; // Player 1 will start
    int movesLeft = 9;
    cout << "Welcome to Tic-Tac-Toe!" << endl;
    while (movesLeft > 0) {
        // Print the board
        cout << endl;
        printBoard(board);
        cout << endl;
        // Determine current player
        char currentPlayer = player1Turn ? 'X' : 'O';
        cout << "Player " << currentPlayer << "'s turn. Enter row (0-2) and column (0-2) separated by
space: ";
        // Get the move
        int row, col;
        cin >> row >> col;
        // Check if the move is valid
        if (row < 0 || row > 2 || col < 0 || col > 2 || board[row][col] != ' ') {
            cout << "Invalid move! Try again." << endl;
            continue;
        }
        // Make the move
        board[row][col] = currentPlayer;
        // Check if someone wins
```

```
        char winner = checkWinner(board);
        if (winner != ' ') {
            cout << endl;
            printBoard(board);
            cout << endl;
            cout << "Player " << winner << " wins!" << endl;
            break;
        }
        // Switch to the other player's turn
        player1Turn = !player1Turn;
        --movesLeft;
    }
    if (movesLeft == 0) {
        cout << endl;
        printBoard(board);
        cout << endl;
        cout << "It's a draw!" << endl;
    }
    return 0;
}
```

6. Memory Match Game

```
#include <iostream>
#include <vector>
#include <cstdlib>
#include <ctime>
#include <algorithm>
using namespace std;
// Function to print the game board
void printBoard(const vector<vector<char>>& board, const vector<vector<bool>>& revealed) {
    cout << "  0 1 2 3" << endl;
    for (int i = 0; i < 4; ++i) {
        cout << i << " ";
        for (int j = 0; j < 4; ++j) {
            if (revealed[i][j]) {
                cout << board[i][j] << " ";
            } else {
                cout << "* ";
            }
        }
        cout << endl;
    }
}
// Function to check if all cards are revealed
bool allRevealed(const vector<vector<bool>>& revealed) {
    for (int i = 0; i < 4; ++i) {
        for (int j = 0; j < 4; ++j) {
            if (!revealed[i][j]) {
                return false;
            }
        }
    }
    return true;
}
int main() {
```

```
srand(time(0)); // Seed the random number generator
vector<vector<char>> board(4, vector<char>(4)); // Initialize empty board
vector<vector<bool>> revealed(4, vector<bool>(4, false)); // Initialize all cards as unrevealed
// Generate a set of letters for the game
vector<char> letters;
for (char ch = 'A'; ch <= 'H'; ++ch) {
  letters.push_back(ch);
  letters.push_back(ch);
}
// Shuffle the letters
random_shuffle(letters.begin(), letters.end());
// Assign the shuffled letters to the board
int index = 0;
for (int i = 0; i < 4; ++i) {
  for (int j = 0; j < 4; ++j) {
    board[i][j] = letters[index++];
  }
}
int moves = 0;
cout << "Welcome to Memory Match!" << endl;
while (!allRevealed(revealed)) {
  cout << endl;
  printBoard(board, revealed);
  cout << endl;
  int row1, col1, row2, col2;
  cout << "Enter the coordinates of the first card (row col): ";
  cin >> row1 >> col1;
  cout << "Enter the coordinates of the second card (row col): ";
  cin >> row2 >> col2;
  if (row1 < 0 || row1 > 3 || col1 < 0 || col1 > 3 || row2 < 0 || row2 > 3 || col2 < 0 || col2 > 3) {
    cout << "Invalid coordinates! Try again." << endl;
    continue;
  }
```

```
        if (revealed[row1][col1] || revealed[row2][col2]) {
            cout << "One or both of the cards have already been revealed! Try again." << endl;
            continue;
        }
        // Reveal the selected cards
        revealed[row1][col1] = true;
        revealed[row2][col2] = true;
        // Print the updated board
        cout << endl;
        printBoard(board, revealed);
        cout << endl;
        // Check if the selected cards match
        if (board[row1][col1] != board[row2][col2]) {
            // If not, hide the cards again after a short delay
            cout << "Sorry, no match! Hiding the cards..." << endl;
            revealed[row1][col1] = false;
            revealed[row2][col2] = false;
        } else {
            cout << "Congratulations, you found a match!" << endl;
        }
        moves++;
    }
    cout << "Congratulations, you've revealed all the cards in " << moves << " moves!" << endl;
    return 0;
}
```

7. Snake Game

```
#include <iostream>
#include <conio.h>
#include <windows.h>
using namespace std;
bool gameOver;
const int width = 20;
const int height = 20;
int x, y, fruitX, fruitY, score;
int tailX[100], tailY[100];
int nTail;
enum eDirection { STOP = 0, LEFT, RIGHT, UP, DOWN };
eDirection dir;
void Setup() {
    gameOver = false;
    dir = STOP;
    x = width / 2;
    y = height / 2;
    fruitX = rand() % width;
    fruitY = rand() % height;
    score = 0;
}
void Draw() {
    system("cls");
    for (int i = 0; i < width + 2; i++)
        cout << "#";
    cout << endl;
    for (int i = 0; i < height; i++) {
        for (int j = 0; j < width; j++) {
            if (j == 0)
                cout << "#";
            if (i == y && j == x)
                cout << "O";
            else if (i == fruitY && j == fruitX)
                cout << "F";
```

```
            else {
                bool print = false;
                for (int k = 0; k < nTail; k++) {
                    if (tailX[k] == j && tailY[k] == i) {
                        cout << "o";
                        print = true;
                    }
                }
                if (!print)
                    cout << " ";
            }
            if (j == width - 1)
                cout << "#";
        }
        cout << endl;
    }
    for (int i = 0; i < width + 2; i++)
        cout << "#";
    cout << endl;
    cout << "Score:" << score << endl;
}
void Input() {
    if (_kbhit()) {
        switch (_getch()) {
        case 'a':
            dir = LEFT;
            break;
        case 'd':
            dir = RIGHT;
            break;
        case 'w':
            dir = UP;
            break;
```

```
        case 's':
            dir = DOWN;
            break;
        case 'x':
            gameOver = true;
            break;
        }
    }
}
void Logic() {
    int prevX = tailX[0];
    int prevY = tailY[0];
    int prev2X, prev2Y;
    tailX[0] = x;
    tailY[0] = y;
    for (int i = 1; i < nTail; i++) {
        prev2X = tailX[i];
        prev2Y = tailY[i];
        tailX[i] = prevX;
        tailY[i] = prevY;
        prevX = prev2X;
        prevY = prev2Y;
    }
    switch (dir) {
    case LEFT:
        x--;
        break;
    case RIGHT:
        x++;
        break;
    case UP:
        y--;
        break;
```

```
  case DOWN:
    y++;
    break;
  default:
    break;
  }
  if (x >= width) x = 0; else if (x < 0) x = width - 1;
  if (y >= height) y = 0; else if (y < 0) y = height - 1;
  for (int i = 0; i < nTail; i++)
    if (tailX[i] == x && tailY[i] == y)
      gameOver = true;
  if (x == fruitX && y == fruitY) {
    score += 10;
    fruitX = rand() % width;
    fruitY = rand() % height;
    nTail++;
  }
}
int main() {
  Setup();
  while (!gameOver) {
    Draw();
    Input();
    Logic();
    Sleep(10); //sleep(10);
  }
  return 0;}
```

8. Pong Game

```
#include <iostream>
#include <conio.h>
#include <windows.h>
using namespace std;
bool gameOver;
const int width = 40;
const int height = 20;
int x, y, fruitX, fruitY, score;
int tailX[100], tailY[100];
int nTail;
enum eDirection { STOP = 0, LEFT, RIGHT, UP, DOWN };
eDirection dir;
void Setup() {
   gameOver = false;
   dir = STOP;
   x = width / 2;
   y = height / 2;
   fruitX = rand() % width;
   fruitY = rand() % height;
   score = 0;
}
void Draw() {
   system("cls");
   for (int i = 0; i < width + 2; i++)
      cout << "#";
   cout << endl;
   for (int i = 0; i < height; i++) {
      for (int j = 0; j < width; j++) {
         if (j == 0)
            cout << "#";
         if (i == y && j == x)
            cout << "O";
         else if (i == fruitY && j == fruitX)
```

```
                cout << "F";
            else {
                bool print = false;
                for (int k = 0; k < nTail; k++) {
                    if (tailX[k] == j && tailY[k] == i) {
                        cout << "o";
                        print = true;
                    }
                }
                if (!print)
                    cout << " ";
            }
            if (j == width - 1)
                cout << "#";
        }
        cout << endl;
    }
    for (int i = 0; i < width + 2; i++)
        cout << "#";
    cout << endl;
    cout << "Score:" << score << endl;
}
void Input() {
    if (_kbhit()) {
        switch (_getch()) {
        case 'a':
            dir = LEFT;
            break;
        case 'd':
            dir = RIGHT;
            break;
        case 'w':
            dir = UP;
            break;
```

```
        case 's':
            dir = DOWN;
            break;
        case 'x':
            gameOver = true;
            break;
        }
    }
}
void Logic() {
    int prevX = tailX[0];
    int prevY = tailY[0];
    int prev2X, prev2Y;
    tailX[0] = x;
    tailY[0] = y;
    for (int i = 1; i < nTail; i++) {
        prev2X = tailX[i];
        prev2Y = tailY[i];
        tailX[i] = prevX;
        tailY[i] = prevY;
        prevX = prev2X;
        prevY = prev2Y;
    }
    switch (dir) {
    case LEFT:
        x--;
        break;
    case RIGHT:
        x++;
        break;
    case UP:
        y--;
        break;
```

```
        case DOWN:
            y++;
            break;
        default:
            break;
        }
        if (x >= width) x = 0; else if (x < 0) x = width - 1;
        if (y >= height) y = 0; else if (y < 0) y = height - 1;

        for (int i = 0; i < nTail; i++)
            if (tailX[i] == x && tailY[i] == y)
                gameOver = true;

        if (x == fruitX && y == fruitY) {
            score += 10;
            fruitX = rand() % width;
            fruitY = rand() % height;
            nTail++;
        }
    }
    int main() {
        Setup();
        while (!gameOver) {
            Draw();
            Input();
            Logic();
            Sleep(10); //sleep(10);
        }
        return 0;
    }
```

9. Brick Breaker Game

```
#include <iostream>
#include <conio.h>
#include <windows.h>
using namespace std;
bool gameOver;
const int width = 30;
const int height = 20;
int x, y, ballX, ballY, score;
int brickX[width * height], brickY[width * height];
int nBricks;
enum eDirection { STOP = 0, LEFT_UP, RIGHT_UP, LEFT_DOWN, RIGHT_DOWN };
eDirection ballDir;
void Setup() {
  gameOver = false;
  x = width / 2;
  y = height - 1;
  ballX = width / 2;
  ballY = height - 2;
  score = 0;
  nBricks = 0;
  for (int i = 0; i < width; i++) {
    for (int j = 0; j < 5; j++) {
      brickX[nBricks] = i;
      brickY[nBricks] = j;
      nBricks++;
    }
  }
  ballDir = LEFT_UP;
}

void Draw() {
  system("cls");
```

```
    for (int i = 0; i < width + 2; i++)
        cout << "#";
    cout << endl;
    for (int i = 0; i < height; i++) {
        for (int j = 0; j < width; j++) {
            if (j == 0)
                cout << "#";
            if ((i == y && j == x) || (i == ballY && j == ballX))
                cout << "O";
            else {
                bool print = false;
                for (int k = 0; k < nBricks; k++) {
                    if (brickX[k] == j && brickY[k] == i) {
                        cout << "X";
                        print = true;
                        break;
                    }
                }
                if (!print)
                    cout << " ";
            }

            if (j == width - 1)
                cout << "#";
        }
        cout << endl;
    }
    for (int i = 0; i < width + 2; i++)
        cout << "#";
    cout << endl;
    cout << "Score:" << score << endl;
}
void Input() {
    if (_kbhit()) {
```

```
            switch (_getch()) {
            case 'a':
                if (x > 0)
                    x--;
                break;
            case 'd':
                if (x < width - 1)
                    x++;
                break;
            case 'x':
                gameOver = true;
                break;
            }
        }
    }
    void Logic() {
        switch (ballDir) {
        case LEFT_UP:
            ballX--;
            ballY--;
            break;
        case RIGHT_UP:
            ballX++;
            ballY--;
            break;
        case LEFT_DOWN:
            ballX--;
            ballY++;
            break;
        case RIGHT_DOWN:
            ballX++;
            ballY++;
            break;
```

```
default:
  break;
}
// Collision with walls
if (ballX <= 0 || ballX >= width - 1) {
  if (ballDir == LEFT_UP)
    ballDir = RIGHT_UP;
  else if (ballDir == LEFT_DOWN)
    ballDir = RIGHT_DOWN;
}
if (ballY <= 0) {
  if (ballDir == LEFT_UP)
    ballDir = LEFT_DOWN;
  else if (ballDir == RIGHT_UP)
    ballDir = RIGHT_DOWN;
}
if (ballY >= height - 1) {
  gameOver = true;
}
// Collision with paddle
if (ballY == y && ballX == x) {
  if (ballDir == LEFT_DOWN)
    ballDir = LEFT_UP;
  else if (ballDir == RIGHT_DOWN)
    ballDir = RIGHT_UP;
}
// Collision with bricks
for (int i = 0; i < nBricks; i++) {
  if (ballX == brickX[i] && ballY == brickY[i]) {
    if (ballDir == LEFT_UP)
      ballDir = LEFT_DOWN;
    else if (ballDir == RIGHT_UP)
      ballDir = RIGHT_DOWN;
    score += 10;
```

```
            brickX[i] = -1; // remove brick
            brickY[i] = -1;
        }
    }
}
int main() {
    Setup();
    while (!gameOver) {
        Draw();
        Input();
        Logic();
        Sleep(50);
    }
    return 0;
}
```

10. Simple Platformer

```
#include <iostream>
#include <conio.h>
#include <windows.h>
using namespace std;
bool gameOver;
const int width = 20;
const int height = 10;
int x, y, score;
enum eDirection { STOP = 0, LEFT, RIGHT };
eDirection dir;
void Setup() {
    gameOver = false;
    dir = STOP;
    x = width / 2;
    y = height - 1;
    score = 0;
}
void Draw() {
    system("cls");
    for (int i = 0; i < width + 2; i++)
        cout << "#";
    cout << endl;
    for (int i = 0; i < height; i++) {
        for (int j = 0; j < width; j++) {
            if (j == 0)
                cout << "#";
            if (i == y && j == x)
                cout << "O";
            else
                cout << " ";
            if (j == width - 1)
                cout << "#";
        }
```

```
            cout << endl;
        }
        for (int i = 0; i < width + 2; i++)
            cout << "#";
        cout << endl;
        cout << "Score:" << score << endl;
    }
    void Input() {
        if (_kbhit()) {
            switch (_getch()) {
            case 'a':
                dir = LEFT;
                break;
            case 'd':
                dir = RIGHT;
                break;
            case 'x':
                gameOver = true;
                break;
            }
        }
    }
    void Logic() {
        switch (dir) {
        case LEFT:
            x--;
            break;
        case RIGHT:
            x++;
            break;
        default:
            break;
        }
        if (x < 0) x = 0;
```

```
    if (x >= width) x = width - 1;
}
int main() {
    Setup();
    while (!gameOver) {
        Draw();
        Input();
        Logic();
        Sleep(50);
    }
    return 0;
}
```

11. Reaction Time Tester

```
#include <iostream>
#include <ctime>
#include <cstdlib>
#include <windows.h>
using namespace std;
int main() {
    cout << "Welcome to Reaction Time Tester!" << endl;
    cout << "Press Enter to start the test." << endl;
    cin.get(); // Wait for the user to press Enter
    // Generate a random delay
    srand(time(0));
    int delay = rand() % 5000 + 1000; // Random delay between 1 and 5 seconds
    // Wait for the delay
    Sleep(delay);
    // Prompt the user to press Enter again
    cout << "Press Enter now!" << endl;
    time_t start = time(0);
    cin.get(); // Wait for the user to press Enter again
    time_t end = time(0);
    // Calculate reaction time
    double reactionTime = difftime(end, start) * 1000; // Convert to milliseconds
    // Display reaction time
    cout << "Your reaction time: " << reactionTime << " milliseconds" << endl;
    return 0;
}
```

12. Whack-a-Mole Game

```
#include <iostream>
#include <ctime>
#include <cstdlib>
#include <conio.h>
#include <windows.h>
using namespace std;
const int width = 10;
const int height = 5;
int score = 0;
bool gameOver = false;
int moleX, moleY;
void Setup() {
   srand(time(0));
   moleX = rand() % width;
   moleY = rand() % height;
}
void Draw() {
   system("cls");
   for (int i = 0; i < width + 2; i++)
      cout << "#";
   cout << endl;
   for (int i = 0; i < height; i++) {
      for (int j = 0; j < width; j++) {
         if (j == 0)
            cout << "#";
         if (i == moleY && j == moleX)
            cout << "M";
         else
            cout << " ";
         if (j == width - 1)
            cout << "#";
      }
      cout << endl;
   }
```

```
    for (int i = 0; i < width + 2; i++)
        cout << "#";
    cout << endl;
    cout << "Score: " << score << endl;
}
void Input() {
    if (_kbhit()) {
        switch (_getch()) {
        case 'a':
            if (moleX > 0)
                moleX--;
            break;
        case 'd':
            if (moleX < width - 1)
                moleX++;
            break;
        case 'w':
            if (moleY > 0)
                moleY--;
            break;
        case 's':
            if (moleY < height - 1)
                moleY++;
            break;
        case 'x':
            gameOver = true;
            break;
        }
    }
}
void Logic() {
    if (moleX == width / 2 && moleY == height / 2) {
        score++;
        moleX = rand() % width;
        moleY = rand() % height;
    }
```

```
}
int main() {
    Setup();
    while (!gameOver) {
        Draw();
        Input();
        Logic();
        Sleep(100);
    }
    return 0;
}
```

13. Number Matching Game

```
#include <iostream>
#include <ctime>
#include <cstdlib>
using namespace std;
int main() {
   srand(time(0)); // Seed the random number generator
   int target = rand() % 100 + 1; // Generate a random number between 1 and 100
   cout << "Welcome to the Number Matching Game!" << endl;
   cout << "Try to guess the number between 1 and 100." << endl;
   int guess;
   int attempts = 0;
   do {
      cout << "Enter your guess: ";
      cin >> guess;
      attempts++;
      if (guess < target) {
         cout << "Too low! Try again." << endl;
      } else if (guess > target) {
         cout << "Too high! Try again." << endl;
      } else {
         cout << "Congratulations! You've guessed the number in " << attempts << " attempts." << endl;
      }
   } while (guess != target);

   return 0;
}
```

14. Card War Game

```
#include <iostream>
#include <vector>
#include <ctime>
#include <cstdlib>
using namespace std;
enum Suit {HEARTS, DIAMONDS, CLUBS, SPADES};
enum Rank {ACE = 1, TWO, THREE, FOUR, FIVE, SIX, SEVEN, EIGHT, NINE, TEN, JACK,
QUEEN, KING};
struct Card {
    Suit suit;
    Rank rank;
};
class Deck {
private:
    vector<Card> cards;
public:
    Deck() {
        for (int s = HEARTS; s <= SPADES; ++s) {
            for (int r = ACE; r <= KING; ++r) {
                Card newCard;
                newCard.suit = static_cast<Suit>(s);
                newCard.rank = static_cast<Rank>(r);
                cards.push_back(newCard);
            }
        }
    }
    void shuffle() {
        srand(time(0));
        for (int i = 0; i < cards.size(); ++i) {
            int j = rand() % cards.size();
            swap(cards[i], cards[j]);
        }
    }
    Card drawCard() {
```

```
        Card drawnCard = cards.back();
        cards.pop_back();
        return drawnCard;
    }
    bool isEmpty() {
        return cards.empty();
    }
};
int main() {
    Deck deck;
    deck.shuffle();
    vector<Card> player1Hand, player2Hand;
    // Distribute cards to players
    while (!deck.isEmpty()) {
        player1Hand.push_back(deck.drawCard());
        player2Hand.push_back(deck.drawCard());
    }
    int player1Score = 0, player2Score = 0;
    // Compare cards
    for (int i = 0; i < player1Hand.size(); ++i) {
        cout << "Player 1's card: " << player1Hand[i].rank << " of ";
        switch (player1Hand[i].suit) {
            case HEARTS:
                cout << "Hearts";
                break;
            case DIAMONDS:
                cout << "Diamonds";
                break;
            case CLUBS:
                cout << "Clubs";
                break;
            case SPADES:
                cout << "Spades";
                break;
```

```
        cout << endl;
        cout << "Player 2's card: " << player2Hand[i].rank << " of ";
        switch (player2Hand[i].suit) {
            case HEARTS:
                cout << "Hearts";
                break;
            case DIAMONDS:
                cout << "Diamonds";
                break;
            case CLUBS:
                cout << "Clubs";
                break;
            case SPADES:
                cout << "Spades";
                break;
        }
        cout << endl;
        if (player1Hand[i].rank > player2Hand[i].rank) {
            cout << "Player 1 wins this round!" << endl;
            player1Score++;
        } else if (player1Hand[i].rank < player2Hand[i].rank) {
            cout << "Player 2 wins this round!" << endl;
            player2Score++;
        } else {
            cout << "It's a tie!" << endl;
        }
        cout << endl;
    }
    cout << "Final Score:" << endl;
    cout << "Player 1: " << player1Score << endl;
    cout << "Player 2: " << player2Score << endl;
    if (player1Score > player2Score) {
        cout << "Player 1 wins!" << endl;
    } else if (player1Score < player2Score) {
        cout << "Player 2 wins!" << endl;
```

```
    } else {
        cout << "It's a tie!" << endl;
    }
    return 0;
}
```

15. Simple RPG Battle

```
#include <iostream>
#include <ctime>
#include <cstdlib>
using namespace std;
class Character {
protected:
    string name;
    int health;
    int attackPower;
public:
    Character(string n, int hp, int atk) : name(n), health(hp), attackPower(atk) {}
    void attack(Character& target) {
        cout << name << " attacks " << target.name << " for " << attackPower << " damage!" <<
endl;
        target.takeDamage(attackPower);
    }
    void takeDamage(int damage) {
        health -= damage;
        if (health <= 0) {
            health = 0;
            cout << name << " has been defeated!" << endl;
        } else {
            cout << name << " takes " << damage << " damage and has " << health << " health
remaining." << endl;
        }
    }
    bool isAlive() {
        return health > 0;
    }
};

class Player : public Character {
public:
    Player(string n, int hp, int atk) : Character(n, hp, atk) {}
```

```
};
class Enemy : public Character {
public:
    Enemy(string n, int hp, int atk) : Character(n, hp, atk) {}
};
int main() {
    srand(time(0));
    Player player("Hero", 100, 20);
    Enemy enemy("Monster", 80, 15);
    cout << "A wild " << enemy.name << " appears!" << endl;
    while (player.isAlive() && enemy.isAlive()) {
        // Player attacks enemy
        player.attack(enemy);
        if (!enemy.isAlive())
            break;
        // Enemy attacks player
        enemy.attack(player);
    }
    cout << "Battle is over!" << endl;
    if (player.isAlive()) {
        cout << "Congratulations! " << player.name << " wins!" << endl;
    } else {
        cout << "Game over! " << player.name << " has been defeated." << endl;
    }
    return 0;
}
```

16. Connect Four Game

```
#include <iostream>
#include <vector>
using namespace std;
const int ROWS = 6;
const int COLS = 7;
const char EMPTY = ' ';
const char PLAYER1 = 'X';
const char PLAYER2 = 'O';
vector<vector<char>> board(ROWS, vector<char>(COLS, EMPTY));
void printBoard() {
    cout << " 1 2 3 4 5 6 7" << endl;
    cout << "---------------" << endl;
    for (int i = 0; i < ROWS; ++i) {
        for (int j = 0; j < COLS; ++j) {
            cout << "|";
            cout << board[i][j];
        }
        cout << "|" << endl;
        cout << "---------------" << endl;
    }
}
bool dropPiece(int col, char player) {
    for (int i = ROWS - 1; i >= 0; --i) {
        if (board[i][col] == EMPTY) {
            board[i][col] = player;
            return true;
        }
    }
    return false;
}
bool checkWin(char player) {
    // Check horizontal
    for (int i = 0; i < ROWS; ++i) {
        for (int j = 0; j < COLS - 3; ++j) {
```

```
            if (board[i][j] == player && board[i][j+1] == player &&
                board[i][j+2] == player && board[i][j+3] == player)
                return true;
        }
    }
    // Check vertical
    for (int i = 0; i < ROWS - 3; ++i) {
        for (int j = 0; j < COLS; ++j) {
            if (board[i][j] == player && board[i+1][j] == player &&
                board[i+2][j] == player && board[i+3][j] == player)
                return true;
        }
    }
    // Check diagonal (down-right)
    for (int i = 0; i < ROWS - 3; ++i) {
        for (int j = 0; j < COLS - 3; ++j) {
            if (board[i][j] == player && board[i+1][j+1] == player &&
                board[i+2][j+2] == player && board[i+3][j+3] == player)
                return true;
        }
    }
    // Check diagonal (up-right)
    for (int i = 3; i < ROWS; ++i) {
        for (int j = 0; j < COLS - 3; ++j) {
            if (board[i][j] == player && board[i-1][j+1] == player &&
                board[i-2][j+2] == player && board[i-3][j+3] == player)
                return true;
        }
    }
    return false;
}
bool isFull() {
    for (int i = 0; i < ROWS; ++i) {
        for (int j = 0; j < COLS; ++j) {
```

```
            if (board[i][j] == EMPTY)
                return false;
        }
    }
    return true;
}
int main() {
    int col;
    char currentPlayer = PLAYER1;
    while (true) {
        printBoard();
        cout << "Player " << currentPlayer << ", enter column (1-7): ";
        cin >> col;
        if (col < 1 || col > 7) {
            cout << "Invalid column. Please enter a number between 1 and 7." << endl;
            continue;
        }
        if (!dropPiece(col - 1, currentPlayer)) {
            cout << "Column is full. Please choose another column." << endl;
            continue;
        }
        if (checkWin(currentPlayer)) {
            printBoard();
            cout << "Player " << currentPlayer << " wins!" << endl;
            break;
        }

        if (isFull()) {
            printBoard();
            cout << "It's a draw!" << endl;
            break;
        }
        currentPlayer = (currentPlayer == PLAYER1) ? PLAYER2 : PLAYER1;
    }   return 0;}
```

17. Battleship Game

```
#include <iostream>
#include <vector>
#include <cstdlib>
#include <ctime>
using namespace std;
const int BOARD_SIZE = 10;
const int NUM_SHIPS = 5;
const char EMPTY = '-';
const char SHIP = 'S';
const char HIT = 'X';
const char MISS = 'O';
vector<vector<char>> playerBoard(BOARD_SIZE, vector<char>(BOARD_SIZE, EMPTY));
vector<vector<char>> computerBoard(BOARD_SIZE, vector<char>(BOARD_SIZE, EMPTY));
struct Ship {
    int size;
    int hits;
};
vector<Ship> ships = {{5, 0}, {4, 0}, {3, 0}, {3, 0}, {2, 0}};
void printBoard(const vector<vector<char>>& board) {
    cout << " ";
    for (int i = 0; i < BOARD_SIZE; ++i)
        cout << " " << i + 1;
    cout << endl;
    for (int i = 0; i < BOARD_SIZE; ++i) {
        cout << char('A' + i) << " ";
        for (int j = 0; j < BOARD_SIZE; ++j)
            cout << board[i][j] << " ";
        cout << endl;
    }
}
bool isValidLocation(int row, int col, int size, bool horizontal, const vector<vector<char>>&
board) {
    if (horizontal) {
        if (col + size > BOARD_SIZE)
```

```
            return false;
        for (int j = col; j < col + size; ++j)
            if (board[row][j] != EMPTY)
                return false;
    } else {
        if (row + size > BOARD_SIZE)
            return false;
        for (int i = row; i < row + size; ++i)
            if (board[i][col] != EMPTY)
                return false;
    }
    return true;
}
void placeShipsRandomly(vector<vector<char>>& board) {
    srand(time(0));
    for (int i = 0; i < NUM_SHIPS; ++i) {
        int row, col;
        bool horizontal;
        do {
            row = rand() % BOARD_SIZE;
            col = rand() % BOARD_SIZE;
            horizontal = rand() % 2 == 0;
        } while (!isValidLocation(row, col, ships[i].size, horizontal, board));

        if (horizontal) {
            for (int j = col; j < col + ships[i].size; ++j)
                board[row][j] = SHIP;
        } else {
            for (int j = row; j < row + ships[i].size; ++j)
                board[j][col] = SHIP;
        }
    }
}
bool isValidInput(string input) {
```

```
    if (input.length() != 2)
        return false;
    char row = input[0], col = input[1];
    return row >= 'A' && row < 'A' + BOARD_SIZE && col >= '1' && col <= '0' + BOARD_SIZE;
}
pair<int, int> parseInput(string input) {
    char row = input[0], col = input[1];
    return {row - 'A', col - '1'};
}
bool isHit(int row, int col, const vector<vector<char>>& board) {
    return board[row][col] == SHIP;
}
void updateBoard(int row, int col, vector<vector<char>>& board) {
    if (isHit(row, col, board))
        board[row][col] = HIT;
    else
        board[row][col] = MISS;
}
bool isSunk(int row, int col, const vector<vector<char>>& board) {
    char direction[] = {-1, 1}; // left and right or up and down
    for (int d : direction) {
        int r = row, c = col, count = 0;
        while (r >= 0 && r < BOARD_SIZE && c >= 0 && c < BOARD_SIZE && board[r][c] ==
HIT) {
            ++count;
            r += d;
        }
        if (count == 5)
            return true;
    }
    return false;
}
int main() {
    cout << "Welcome to Battleship!" << endl;
```

```
    cout << "Player and Computer's boards:" << endl;
    printBoard(playerBoard);
    printBoard(computerBoard);
    placeShipsRandomly(computerBoard);
    int playerShipsLeft = NUM_SHIPS, computerShipsLeft = NUM_SHIPS;
    while (playerShipsLeft > 0 && computerShipsLeft > 0) {
        string input;
        cout << "Enter your shot (e.g., A1): ";
        cin >> input;
        if (!isValidInput(input)) {
            cout << "Invalid input! Please enter a valid coordinate (e.g., A1)." << endl;
            continue;
        }
        pair<int, int> target = parseInput(input);
        int row = target.first, col = target.second;
        if (computerBoard[row][col] == HIT || computerBoard[row][col] == MISS) {
            cout << "You've already fired at this location!" << endl;
            continue;
        }
        if (isHit(row, col, computerBoard)) {
            cout << "You hit a ship!" << endl;
            updateBoard(row, col, computerBoard);
            if (isSunk(row, col, computerBoard)) {
                cout << "You've sunk the enemy ship!" << endl;
                --computerShipsLeft;
            }
        } else {
            cout << "You missed!" << endl;
            updateBoard(row, col, computerBoard);
        }
        cout << "Computer's turn:" << endl;
        int computerRow, computerCol;
        do {
            computerRow = rand() % BOARD_SIZE;
```

```
            computerCol = rand() % BOARD_SIZE;
        } while (playerBoard[computerRow][computerCol] == HIT ||
playerBoard[computerRow][computerCol] == MISS);
        if (isHit(computerRow, computerCol, playerBoard)) {
            cout << "Computer hit your ship!" << endl;
            updateBoard(computerRow, computerCol, playerBoard);
            if (isSunk(computerRow, computerCol, playerBoard)) {
                cout << "Computer has sunk your ship!" << endl;
                --playerShipsLeft;
            }
        } else {
            cout << "Computer missed!" << endl;
            updateBoard(computerRow, computerCol, playerBoard);
        }
        cout << "Player and Computer's boards:" << endl;
        printBoard(playerBoard);
        printBoard(computerBoard);
        cout << "Player's ships left: " << playerShipsLeft << endl;
        cout << "Computer's ships left: " << computerShipsLeft << endl;
    }

    if (playerShipsLeft == 0)
        cout << "Computer wins!" << endl;
    else
        cout << "Player wins!" << endl;
    return 0;
}
```

18. Simple Blackjack

```
#include <iostream>
#include <vector>
#include <ctime>
#include <cstdlib>
using namespace std;
enum class Suit { HEARTS, DIAMONDS, CLUBS, SPADES };
enum class Rank { ACE = 1, TWO, THREE, FOUR, FIVE, SIX, SEVEN, EIGHT, NINE, TEN,
JACK, QUEEN, KING };
struct Card {
  Suit suit;
  Rank rank;
};
class Deck {
private:
  vector<Card> cards;
public:
  Deck() {
    for (int s = static_cast<int>(Suit::HEARTS); s <= static_cast<int>(Suit::SPADES); ++s) {
      for (int r = static_cast<int>(Rank::ACE); r <= static_cast<int>(Rank::KING); ++r) {
        Card newCard;
        newCard.suit = static_cast<Suit>(s);
        newCard.rank = static_cast<Rank>(r);
        cards.push_back(newCard);
      }
    }
  }
  void shuffle() {
    srand(time(0));
    for (int i = 0; i < cards.size(); ++i) {
      int j = rand() % cards.size();
      swap(cards[i], cards[j]);
    }
  }
  Card drawCard() {
```

```
        Card drawnCard = cards.back();
        cards.pop_back();
        return drawnCard;
    }
};
int main() {
    Deck deck;
    deck.shuffle();
    int playerScore = 0, dealerScore = 0;
    // Initial deal
    playerScore += static_cast<int>(deck.drawCard().rank);
    dealerScore += static_cast<int>(deck.drawCard().rank);
    // Player's turn
    char choice;
    do {
        cout << "Your current score: " << playerScore << endl;
        cout << "Hit (h) or Stand (s)? ";
        cin >> choice;
        if (choice == 'h') {
            playerScore += static_cast<int>(deck.drawCard().rank);
            if (playerScore > 21) {
                cout << "Bust! You lose." << endl;
                return 0;
            }
        }
    } while (choice == 'h');
    // Dealer's turn
    while (dealerScore < 17) {
        dealerScore += static_cast<int>(deck.drawCard().rank);
        if (dealerScore > 21) {
            cout << "Dealer busts! You win." << endl;
            return 0;
        }
    }
```

```
    // Compare scores
    cout << "Your score: " << playerScore << endl;
    cout << "Dealer's score: " << dealerScore << endl;
    if (playerScore > dealerScore)
        cout << "You win!" << endl;
    else if (dealerScore > playerScore)
        cout << "Dealer wins!" << endl;
    else
        cout << "It's a tie!" << endl;
    return 0;
}
```

19. Space Invaders (Text-based)

```
#include <iostream>
#include <vector>
#include <cstdlib>
#include <ctime>
#include <conio.h>
#include <windows.h>
using namespace std;
const int WIDTH = 40;
const int HEIGHT = 20;
const char SHIP = '^';
const char INVADER = 'V';
const char MISSILE = '|';
bool gameOver;
int shipX, invaderX, invaderY;
vector<pair<int, int>> missiles;
void Setup() {
  gameOver = false;
  shipX = WIDTH / 2;
  invaderX = rand() % WIDTH;
  invaderY = 0;
}
void Draw() {
  system("cls");
  for (int i = 0; i < WIDTH + 2; i++)
    cout << "#";
  cout << endl;
  for (int i = 0; i < HEIGHT; i++) {
    for (int j = 0; j < WIDTH; j++) {
      if (j == 0)
        cout << "#";
      if (i == 0 && j == shipX)
        cout << SHIP;
      else if (i == invaderY && j == invaderX)
        cout << INVADER;
```

```
            else {
                bool missileFound = false;
                for (auto missile : missiles) {
                    if (missile.first == i && missile.second == j) {
                        cout << MISSILE;
                        missileFound = true;
                    }
                }
                if (!missileFound)
                    cout << " ";
            }
            if (j == WIDTH - 1)
                cout << "#";
        }
        cout << endl;
    }
    for (int i = 0; i < WIDTH + 2; i++)
        cout << "#";
    cout << endl;
}
void Input() {
    if (_kbhit()) {
        switch (_getch()) {
        case 'a':
            if (shipX > 0)
                shipX--;
            break;
        case 'd':
            if (shipX < WIDTH - 1)
                shipX++;
            break;
        case 'x':
            gameOver = true;
            break;
```

```
            case ' ':
                missiles.push_back(make_pair(HEIGHT - 1, shipX));
                break;
            }
        }
    }
    void Logic() {
        // Move invader down
        invaderY++;
        // Move missiles
        for (int i = 0; i < missiles.size(); i++) {
            missiles[i].first--;
            if (missiles[i].first == invaderY && missiles[i].second == invaderX) {
                // Invader hit
                invaderX = rand() % WIDTH;
                invaderY = 0;
                missiles.erase(missiles.begin() + i);
            }
        }
        // Check for game over
        for (auto missile : missiles) {
            if (missile.first == 0 && missile.second == invaderX) {
                gameOver = true;
                break;
            }
        }
    }

    int main() {
        srand(time(0));
        Setup();
        while (!gameOver) {
            Draw();
            Input();
```

```
        Logic();
        Sleep(100);
    }
    cout << "Game Over!" << endl;
    return 0;
}
```

20. Trivia Quiz Game

```
#include <iostream>
#include <vector>
#include <string>
using namespace std;
struct Question {
    string question;
    vector<string> options;
    int correctOption;
};
int main() {
    vector<Question> questions = {
        {"What is the capital of France?", {"London", "Paris", "Berlin", "Rome"}, 2},
        {"What is the largest mammal?", {"Elephant", "Blue Whale", "Giraffe", "Hippopotamus"},
1},
        {"Which planet is known as the Red Planet?", {"Venus", "Mars", "Jupiter", "Saturn"}, 1},
        {"What is the chemical symbol for water?", {"H2O", "CO2", "O2", "H2SO4"}, 0},
        {"Who wrote 'Romeo and Juliet'?", {"Charles Dickens", "Jane Austen", "William
Shakespeare", "Mark Twain"}, 2}
    };
    int score = 0;
    for (int i = 0; i < questions.size(); ++i) {
        cout << "Question " << i + 1 << ": " << questions[i].question << endl;
        cout << "Options:" << endl;
        for (int j = 0; j < questions[i].options.size(); ++j) {
            cout << j + 1 << ". " << questions[i].options[j] << endl;
        }
        int answer;
        cout << "Enter your answer (1-4): ";
        cin >> answer;
        if (answer == questions[i].correctOption + 1) {
            cout << "Correct!" << endl;
            ++score;
        } else {
            cout << "Incorrect. The correct answer is: " <<
```

```
questions[i].options[questions[i].correctOption] << endl;
        }
        cout << endl;
    }
    cout << "Quiz complete!" << endl;
    cout << "Your score: " << score << "/" << questions.size() << endl;
    return 0;
}
```

21. Falling Blocks Game

```
#include <iostream>
#include <cstdlib>
#include <ctime>
#include <conio.h>
#include <windows.h>
using namespace std;
const int WIDTH = 10;
const int HEIGHT = 20;
const char BLOCK = '*';
const char EMPTY = ' ';
const int TICK_RATE = 500; // milliseconds
bool gameOver;
int score;
char board[HEIGHT][WIDTH];
struct Block {
   int x, y;
} currentBlock;
void Setup() {
   gameOver = false;
   score = 0;
   for (int i = 0; i < HEIGHT; ++i)
      for (int j = 0; j < WIDTH; ++j)
         board[i][j] = EMPTY;
}
void Draw() {
   system("cls");
   for (int i = 0; i < WIDTH + 2; i++)
      cout << "#";
   cout << endl;
   for (int i = 0; i < HEIGHT; i++) {
      for (int j = 0; j < WIDTH; j++) {
         if (j == 0)
            cout << "#";
         if (i == currentBlock.y && j == currentBlock.x)
```

```
                cout << BLOCK;
            else
                cout << board[i][j];
            if (j == WIDTH - 1)
                cout << "#";
        }
        cout << endl;
    }
    for (int i = 0; i < WIDTH + 2; i++)
        cout << "#";
    cout << endl;
    cout << "Score: " << score << endl;
}
void Input() {
    if (_kbhit()) {
        switch (_getch()) {
        case 'a':
            if (currentBlock.x > 0)
                currentBlock.x--;
            break;
        case 'd':
            if (currentBlock.x < WIDTH - 1)
                currentBlock.x++;
            break;
        case 'x':
            gameOver = true;
            break;
        }
    }
}
bool IsValidPosition() {
    return currentBlock.y < HEIGHT && board[currentBlock.y][currentBlock.x] == EMPTY;
}
void AddBlockToBoard() {
```

```
      board[currentBlock.y][currentBlock.x] = BLOCK;
   }
   void RemoveCompletedRows() {
      for (int i = HEIGHT - 1; i >= 0; i--) {
         bool isRowCompleted = true;
         for (int j = 0; j < WIDTH; j++) {
            if (board[i][j] == EMPTY) {
               isRowCompleted = false;
               break;
            }
         }
         if (isRowCompleted) {
            for (int k = i; k > 0; k--) {
               for (int j = 0; j < WIDTH; j++) {
                  board[k][j] = board[k - 1][j];
               }
            }
            score++;
            i++; // Recheck the current row after shifting rows down
         }
      }
   }
   void MoveBlockDown() {
      currentBlock.y++;
   }
   void Update() {
      if (!IsValidPosition()) {
         AddBlockToBoard();
         RemoveCompletedRows();
         currentBlock.x = rand() % WIDTH;
         currentBlock.y = 0;
         if (!IsValidPosition()) {
            gameOver = true;
            return;
```

```
        }
    }
    MoveBlockDown();
}
int main() {
    srand(time(0));
    Setup();
    while (!gameOver) {
        Draw();
        Input();
        Update();
        Sleep(TICK_RATE);
    }
    cout << "Game Over! Your score: " << score << endl;
    return 0;
}
```

22. Simple Racing Game

```
#include <iostream>
#include <cstdlib>
#include <ctime>
#include <conio.h>
#include <windows.h>
using namespace std;
const int TRACK_WIDTH = 20;
const int CAR_WIDTH = 3;
const int TICK_RATE = 100; // milliseconds
bool gameOver;
int carPosition;
int obstaclePosition;
void Setup() {
    gameOver = false;
    carPosition = TRACK_WIDTH / 2;
    obstaclePosition = rand() % TRACK_WIDTH;
}
void Draw() {
    system("cls");
    for (int i = 0; i < TRACK_WIDTH + 2; i++)
        cout << "#";
    cout << endl;
    for (int i = 0; i < TRACK_WIDTH; i++) {
        if (i == 0)
            cout << "#";
        if (i == carPosition)
            cout << ">";
        else if (i == obstaclePosition)
            cout << "X";
        else
            cout << " ";
        if (i == TRACK_WIDTH - 1)
            cout << "#";
    }
```

```
    cout << endl;
    for (int i = 0; i < TRACK_WIDTH + 2; i++)
        cout << "#";
    cout << endl;
    cout << "Press 'a' to move left, 'd' to move right, and 'x' to quit." << endl;
}
void Input() {
    if (_kbhit()) {
        switch (_getch()) {
        case 'a':
            if (carPosition > 0)
                carPosition--;
            break;
        case 'd':
            if (carPosition < TRACK_WIDTH - CAR_WIDTH)
                carPosition++;
            break;
        case 'x':
            gameOver = true;
            break;
        }
    }
}
void Update() {
    obstaclePosition = (obstaclePosition + 1) % TRACK_WIDTH;
    if (obstaclePosition >= carPosition && obstaclePosition < carPosition + CAR_WIDTH) {
        gameOver = true;
    }
}
int main() {
    srand(time(0));
    Setup();
    while (!gameOver) {
        Draw();
```

```
        Input();
        Update();
        Sleep(TICK_RATE);
    }
    cout << "Game Over!" << endl;
    return 0;
}
```

23. Word Search Puzzle

```
#include <iostream>
#include <vector>
#include <string>
#include <ctime>
#include <cstdlib>
using namespace std;
const int ROWS = 10;
const int COLS = 10;
const string words[] = {"HELLO", "WORLD", "PYTHON", "PROGRAMMING",
"LANGUAGE"};
const int numWords = sizeof(words) / sizeof(words[0]);
const char EMPTY = '.';
const char FILLED = '*';
vector<vector<char>> grid(ROWS, vector<char>(COLS, EMPTY));
void initializeGrid() {
   srand(time(0));
   for (int i = 0; i < numWords; ++i) {
      string word = words[i];
      int len = word.length();
      int row = rand() % ROWS;
      int col = rand() % (COLS - len + 1);
      bool placed = false;
      // Try to place word horizontally
      if (col + len <= COLS) {
         placed = true;
         for (int j = 0; j < len; ++j) {
            if (grid[row][col + j] != EMPTY && grid[row][col + j] != word[j]) {
               placed = false;
               break;
            }
         }
         if (placed) {
            for (int j = 0; j < len; ++j)
               grid[row][col + j] = word[j];
```

```
            }
        }
        // If horizontal placement fails, try vertical placement
        if (!placed) {
            col = rand() % COLS;
            row = rand() % (ROWS - len + 1);
            if (row + len <= ROWS) {
                placed = true;
                for (int j = 0; j < len; ++j) {
                    if (grid[row + j][col] != EMPTY && grid[row + j][col] != word[j]) {
                        placed = false;
                        break;
                    }
                }
                if (placed) {
                    for (int j = 0; j < len; ++j)
                        grid[row + j][col] = word[j];
                }
            }
        }
    }
    // Fill remaining empty cells with random characters
    for (int i = 0; i < ROWS; ++i) {
        for (int j = 0; j < COLS; ++j) {
            if (grid[i][j] == EMPTY)
                grid[i][j] = 'A' + rand() % 26; // Random uppercase letter
        }
    }
}
void printGrid() {
    for (int i = 0; i < ROWS; ++i) {
        for (int j = 0; j < COLS; ++j) {
            cout << grid[i][j] << " ";
        }
```

```
            cout << endl;
        }
    }
    bool searchWord(const string& word) {
        // Search horizontally
        for (int i = 0; i < ROWS; ++i) {
            for (int j = 0; j <= COLS - word.length(); ++j) {
                bool found = true;
                for (int k = 0; k < word.length(); ++k) {
                    if (grid[i][j + k] != word[k]) {
                        found = false;
                        break;
                    }
                }
                if (found)
                    return true;
            }
        }
        // Search vertically
        for (int j = 0; j < COLS; ++j) {
            for (int i = 0; i <= ROWS - word.length(); ++i) {
                bool found = true;
                for (int k = 0; k < word.length(); ++k) {
                    if (grid[i + k][j] != word[k]) {
                        found = false;
                        break;
                    }
                }
                if (found)
                    return true;
            }
        }
        return false;
    }
```

```
int main() {
    initializeGrid();
    printGrid();
    cout << "Words to find:" << endl;
    for (int i = 0; i < numWords; ++i)
        cout << words[i] << endl;
    cout << "Enter a word to search (type 'q' to quit): ";
    string word;
    while (cin >> word) {
        if (word == "q")
            break;
        if (searchWord(word))
            cout << "Word found!" << endl;
        else
            cout << "Word not found." << endl;

        cout << "Enter a word to search (type 'q' to quit): ";
    }
    return 0;
}
```

24. Simple Chess Game

```
#include <iostream>
#include <vector>
#include <string>
#include <cctype>
using namespace std;
const int BOARD_SIZE = 8;
// Enum for the pieces
enum class Piece { EMPTY, PAWN, ROOK, KNIGHT, BISHOP, QUEEN, KING };
// Struct to represent a position on the board
struct Position {
   int row;
   int col;
};
// Struct to represent a move
struct Move {
   Position from;
   Position to;
};
// Struct to represent a chess piece
struct ChessPiece {
   Piece piece;
   bool isWhite;
};
// Function to initialize the chess board
vector<vector<ChessPiece>> initBoard() {
   vector<vector<ChessPiece>> board(BOARD_SIZE, vector<ChessPiece>(BOARD_SIZE,
{Piece::EMPTY, false}));
   // Initialize white pieces
   board[0][0] = {Piece::ROOK, true};
   board[0][1] = {Piece::KNIGHT, true};
   board[0][2] = {Piece::BISHOP, true};
   board[0][3] = {Piece::QUEEN, true};
   board[0][4] = {Piece::KING, true};
   board[0][5] = {Piece::BISHOP, true};
```

```
        board[0][6] = {Piece::KNIGHT, true};
        board[0][7] = {Piece::ROOK, true};
        for (int i = 0; i < BOARD_SIZE; ++i) {
            board[1][i] = {Piece::PAWN, true};
        }
        // Initialize black pieces
        board[7][0] = {Piece::ROOK, false};
        board[7][1] = {Piece::KNIGHT, false};
        board[7][2] = {Piece::BISHOP, false};
        board[7][3] = {Piece::QUEEN, false};
        board[7][4] = {Piece::KING, false};
        board[7][5] = {Piece::BISHOP, false};
        board[7][6] = {Piece::KNIGHT, false};
        board[7][7] = {Piece::ROOK, false};
        for (int i = 0; i < BOARD_SIZE; ++i) {
            board[6][i] = {Piece::PAWN, false};
        }
        return board;
    }
    // Function to print the chess board
    void printBoard(const vector<vector<ChessPiece>>& board) {
        cout << "   a b c d e f g h" << endl;
        cout << "  -----------------" << endl;
        for (int i = 0; i < BOARD_SIZE; ++i) {
            cout << 8 - i << "| ";
            for (int j = 0; j < BOARD_SIZE; ++j) {
                switch (board[i][j].piece) {
                    case Piece::EMPTY:
                        cout << ". ";
                        break;
                    case Piece::PAWN:
                        cout << (board[i][j].isWhite ? "P" : "p") << " ";
                        break;
                    case Piece::ROOK:
```

```
                cout << (board[i][j].isWhite ? "R" : "r") << " ";
                break;
            case Piece::KNIGHT:
                cout << (board[i][j].isWhite ? "N" : "n") << " ";
                break;
            case Piece::BISHOP:
                cout << (board[i][j].isWhite ? "B" : "b") << " ";
                break;
            case Piece::QUEEN:
                cout << (board[i][j].isWhite ? "Q" : "q") << " ";
                break;
            case Piece::KING:
                cout << (board[i][j].isWhite ? "K" : "k") << " ";
                break;
        }
    }
    cout << "|" << endl;
  }
  cout << "  -----------------" << endl;
}
// Function to check if a position is valid on the board
bool isValidPosition(const Position& pos) {
  return pos.row >= 0 && pos.row < BOARD_SIZE && pos.col >= 0 && pos.col <
BOARD_SIZE;
}
// Function to check if a move is valid
bool isValidMove(const vector<vector<ChessPiece>>& board, const Move& move, bool
isWhiteTurn) {
  // Check if positions are valid
  if (!isValidPosition(move.from) || !isValidPosition(move.to))
    return false;
  // Check if the piece belongs to the player whose turn it is
  if (board[move.from.row][move.from.col].isWhite != isWhiteTurn)
    return false;
```

```
        // Check if the destination is not occupied by a friendly piece
        if (board[move.to.row][move.to.col].isWhite == isWhiteTurn)
            return false;
        // Additional logic for piece-specific moves can be added here
        return true;
    }
    int main() {
        vector<vector<ChessPiece>> board = initBoard();
        printBoard(board);
        bool isWhiteTurn = true;
        while (true) {
            string player = isWhiteTurn ? "White" : "Black";
            cout << player << "'s turn. Enter move (e.g., e2 e4): ";
            string from, to;
            cin >> from >> to;
            // Convert user input to positions
            Position fromPos = {BOARD_SIZE - (from[1] - '0'), from[0] - 'a'};
            Position toPos = {BOARD_SIZE - (to[1] - '0'), to[0] - 'a'};
            Move move = {fromPos, toPos};
            // Validate and perform the move
            if (isValidMove(board, move, isWhiteTurn)) {
                board[toPos.row][toPos.col] = board[fromPos.row][fromPos.col];
                board[fromPos.row][fromPos.col] = {Piece::EMPTY, false};
                printBoard(board);
                isWhiteTurn = !isWhiteTurn; // Switch turns
            } else {
                cout << "Invalid move. Try again." << endl;
            }
        }
        return 0;
    }
```

25. Mastermind Game

```
#include <iostream>
#include <vector>
#include <cstdlib>
#include <ctime>
using namespace std;
const int CODE_LENGTH = 4;
const int NUM_COLORS = 6;
const int NUM_ATTEMPTS = 10;
// Function to generate a random secret code
vector<int> generateSecretCode() {
    vector<int> code(CODE_LENGTH);
    srand(time(0));
    for (int i = 0; i < CODE_LENGTH; ++i) {
        code[i] = rand() % NUM_COLORS;
    }
    return code;
}
// Function to input a guess from the player
vector<int> inputGuess() {
    vector<int> guess(CODE_LENGTH);
    cout << "Enter your guess (0-" << NUM_COLORS - 1 << ") for each position: ";
    for (int i = 0; i < CODE_LENGTH; ++i) {
        cin >> guess[i];
    }
    return guess;
}
// Function to check the correctness of the guess
pair<int, int> checkGuess(const vector<int>& secretCode, const vector<int>& guess) {
    int numCorrect = 0; // Number of correct colors in correct positions
    int numMisplaced = 0; // Number of correct colors in incorrect positions
    vector<bool> secretVisited(CODE_LENGTH, false); // To track which positions have been
matched in the secret code
    vector<bool> guessVisited(CODE_LENGTH, false); // To track which positions have been
matched in the guess
```

```
        // First pass: Check for correct colors in correct positions
        for (int i = 0; i < CODE_LENGTH; ++i) {
            if (secretCode[i] == guess[i]) {
                numCorrect++;
                secretVisited[i] = true;
                guessVisited[i] = true;
            }
        }
        // Second pass: Check for correct colors in incorrect positions
        for (int i = 0; i < CODE_LENGTH; ++i) {
            if (!secretVisited[i]) {
                for (int j = 0; j < CODE_LENGTH; ++j) {
                    if (!guessVisited[j] && secretCode[i] == guess[j]) {
                        numMisplaced++;
                        secretVisited[i] = true;
                        guessVisited[j] = true;
                        break;
                    }
                }
            }
        }
        return make_pair(numCorrect, numMisplaced);
    }
    int main() {
        cout << "Welcome to Mastermind!" << endl;
        cout << "Guess the secret code of " << CODE_LENGTH << " colors, each between 0 and " <<
    NUM_COLORS - 1 << "." << endl;
        cout << "You have " << NUM_ATTEMPTS << " attempts." << endl;

        vector<int> secretCode = generateSecretCode();
        int attempt = 0;
        while (attempt < NUM_ATTEMPTS) {
            cout << "Attempt " << attempt + 1 << "/" << NUM_ATTEMPTS << ":" << endl;
            vector<int> guess = inputGuess();
```

```
        pair<int, int> result = checkGuess(secretCode, guess);
        cout << "Result: " << result.first << " correct color(s) in correct position, ";
        cout << result.second << " correct color(s) in incorrect position." << endl;
        if (result.first == CODE_LENGTH) {
            cout << "Congratulations! You guessed the secret code!" << endl;
            break;
        }
        attempt++;
    }
    if (attempt == NUM_ATTEMPTS) {
        cout << "Sorry, you've run out of attempts. The secret code was:";
        for (int i = 0; i < CODE_LENGTH; ++i) {
            cout << " " << secretCode[i];
        }
        cout << endl;
    }
    return 0;
}
```

26. Text-Based RPG Adventure

```
#include <iostream>
#include <string>
#include <ctime>
#include <cstdlib>
using namespace std;
// Player class
class Player {
private:
    string name;
    int health;
    int damage;
    int gold;
public:
    Player(string playerName) {
        name = playerName;
        health = 100;
        damage = 10;
        gold = 0;
    }
    // Getters
    string getName() const {
        return name;
    }
    int getHealth() const {
        return health;
    }
    int getGold() const {
        return gold;
    }
    // Methods
    void attack() {
        cout << "You attack the enemy!" << endl;
    }
    void takeDamage(int amount) {
```

```
        health -= amount;
        if (health <= 0) {
            health = 0;
            cout << "You have been defeated!" << endl;
        }
    }
    void gainGold(int amount) {
        gold += amount;
        cout << "You found " << amount << " gold!" << endl;
    }
    bool isAlive() const {
        return health > 0;
    }
};
// Enemy class
class Enemy {
private:
    string name;
    int health;
    int damage;
    int goldReward;
public:
    Enemy(string enemyName, int enemyHealth, int enemyDamage, int reward) {
        name = enemyName;
        health = enemyHealth;
        damage = enemyDamage;
        goldReward = reward;
    }
    // Methods
    void attack(Player& player) {
        cout << "The " << name << " attacks you!" << endl;
        player.takeDamage(damage);
    }
    bool isAlive() const {
```

```
        return health > 0;
    }
    int getGoldReward() const {
        return goldReward;
    }
};
// Function to simulate a battle between the player and an enemy
void battle(Player& player, Enemy& enemy) {
    cout << "You encountered a " << enemy.getName() << "!" << endl;
    while (player.isAlive() && enemy.isAlive()) {
        // Player's turn
        player.attack();
        enemy.takeDamage(player.getDamage());
        // Enemy's turn
        if (enemy.isAlive()) {
            enemy.attack(player);
        }
    }
    // If player wins, gain gold reward
    if (player.isAlive()) {
        player.gainGold(enemy.getGoldReward());
    }
}
// Function to simulate the RPG adventure
void adventure(Player& player) {
    cout << "Welcome, " << player.getName() << ", to the RPG Adventure!" << endl;
    cout << "Your quest begins..." << endl;
    // Simulate random encounters
    srand(time(0));
    for (int i = 1; i <= 3; ++i) {
        cout << "----- Encounter " << i << " -----" << endl;
        Enemy enemy("Goblin", 30, 8, 20); // Example enemy (name, health, damage, gold reward)
        battle(player, enemy);
        if (!player.isAlive()) {
```

```
            cout << "Game over! You were defeated." << endl;
            return;
        }
    }
    // End of adventure
    cout << "Congratulations, " << player.getName() << "! You have completed the RPG
adventure!" << endl;
    cout << "You collected " << player.getGold() << " gold during your journey." << endl;
}
int main() {
    string playerName;
    cout << "Enter your name: ";
    cin >> playerName;
    Player player(playerName);
    adventure(player);
    return 0;
}
```

27. Simple Simon Game

```
#include <iostream>
#include <vector>
#include <cstdlib>
#include <ctime>
#include <windows.h>
using namespace std;
const int MAX_MOVES = 10;
const int DELAY_MS = 1000;
// Function to generate a random move (0 = red, 1 = green, 2 = blue, 3 = yellow)
int generateMove() {
    return rand() % 4;
}
// Function to display a color for a certain duration
void displayColor(int color) {
    switch (color) {
        case 0: // red
            cout << "Red" << endl;
            break;
        case 1: // green
            cout << "Green" << endl;
            break;
        case 2: // blue
            cout << "Blue" << endl;
            break;
        case 3: // yellow
            cout << "Yellow" << endl;
            break;
    }
    Sleep(DELAY_MS); // pause for a moment to display the color
    system("cls"); // clear the screen
}
// Function to play the game
bool playSimonGame() {
```

```
    vector<int> sequence; // stores the sequence of moves
    vector<int> playerMoves; // stores the player's moves
    cout << "Welcome to Simple Simon! Remember the sequence and repeat it." << endl;
    cout << "The colors are represented by numbers: 0 = Red, 1 = Green, 2 = Blue, 3 = Yellow" <<
endl;
    // Generate the sequence of moves
    for (int i = 0; i < MAX_MOVES; ++i) {
        int move = generateMove();
        sequence.push_back(move);
        displayColor(move);
    }
    cout << "Your turn! Enter the sequence of colors (each color represented by a number):" <<
endl;
    // Get the player's moves
    for (int i = 0; i < MAX_MOVES; ++i) {
        int move;
        cin >> move;
        playerMoves.push_back(move);
    }
    // Check if the player's sequence matches the generated sequence
    for (int i = 0; i < MAX_MOVES; ++i) {
        if (playerMoves[i] != sequence[i]) {
            cout << "Incorrect sequence. Game over!" << endl;
            return false;
        }
    }
    cout << "Congratulations! You remembered the sequence correctly!" << endl;
    return true;
}
int main() {
    srand(time(0)); // seed the random number generator
    char playAgain;
    do {
        if (!playSimonGame()) {
```

```
            break; // exit the loop if the player loses
        }
        cout << "Do you want to play again? (y/n): ";
        cin >> playAgain;
    } while (playAgain == 'y' || playAgain == 'Y');
    cout << "Thanks for playing Simple Simon!" << endl;
    return 0;
}
```

28. Frogger-style Game

```
#include <iostream>
#include <cstdlib>
#include <conio.h>
#include <ctime>
#include <windows.h>
using namespace std;
const int WIDTH = 20;
const int HEIGHT = 10;
const char FROG = 'O';
const char LOG = '-';
const char CAR = '#';
const int TICK_RATE = 200; // milliseconds
bool gameOver;
int frogX, frogY;
int carX, carY;
int logX, logY;
void Setup() {
    gameOver = false;
    frogX = WIDTH / 2;
    frogY = HEIGHT - 1;
    carX = rand() % WIDTH;
    carY = rand() % HEIGHT;
    logX = rand() % WIDTH;
    logY = rand() % HEIGHT;
}
void Draw() {
    system("cls");
    for (int i = 0; i < WIDTH + 2; i++)
        cout << "#";
    cout << endl;
    for (int i = 0; i < HEIGHT; i++) {
        for (int j = 0; j < WIDTH; j++) {
            if (j == 0 || j == WIDTH - 1)
                cout << "#";
```

```
            else if (i == frogY && j == frogX)
                cout << FROG;
            else if (i == carY && j == carX)
                cout << CAR;
            else if (i == logY && j == logX)
                cout << LOG;
            else
                cout << " ";
        }
        cout << endl;
    }
    for (int i = 0; i < WIDTH + 2; i++)
        cout << "#";
    cout << endl;
}
void Input() {
    if (_kbhit()) {
        switch (_getch()) {
        case 'a':
            if (frogX > 1)
                frogX--;
            break;
        case 'd':
            if (frogX < WIDTH - 2)
                frogX++;
            break;
        case 'w':
            if (frogY > 0)
                frogY--;
            break;
        case 's':
            if (frogY < HEIGHT - 1)
                frogY++;
            break;
```

```
            case 'x':
                gameOver = true;
                break;
            }
        }
    }
    void Update() {
        // Move the car left
        carX--;
        if (carX < 0)
            carX = WIDTH - 1;
        // Move the log right
        logX++;
        if (logX >= WIDTH)
            logX = 0;
        // Check for collision with car
        if (frogX == carX && frogY == carY)
            gameOver = true;
        // Check for collision with log
        if (frogX == logX && frogY == logY)
            frogX++; // move frog with the log
    }
    int main() {
        srand(time(0));
        Setup();
        while (!gameOver) {
            Draw();
            Input();
            Update();
            Sleep(TICK_RATE);
        }
        cout << "Game Over!" << endl;
        return 0;
    }
```

29. Hangman with Graphics

```
#include <iostream>
#include <string>
#include <vector>
using namespace std;
const vector<string> hangmanDrawing = {
    " +---+\n"
    " |  |\n"
    "    |\n"
    "    |\n"
    "    |\n"
    "    |\n"
    "=========\n",
    " +---+\n"
    " |  |\n"
    " O  |\n"
    "    |\n"
    "    |\n"
    "    |\n"
    "=========\n",
    " +---+\n"
    " |  |\n"
    " O  |\n"
    " |  |\n"
    "    |\n"
    "    |\n"
    "=========\n",
    " +---+\n"
    " |  |\n"
    " O  |\n"
    "/|  |\n"
    "    |\n"
    "    |\n"
    "=========\n",
    " +---+\n"
```

```
    " |   |\n"
    " O   |\n"
    " /|\\ |\n"
    "     |\n"
    "     |\n"
    "=========\n",
    " +---+\n"
    " |   |\n"
    " O   |\n"
    " /|\\ |\n"
    " /   |\n"
    "     |\n"
    "=========\n",
    " +---+\n"
    " |   |\n"
    " O   |\n"
    " /|\\ |\n"
    " / \\ |\n"
    "     |\n"
    "=========\n"
};
// Function to display hangman graphics based on the number of incorrect guesses
void displayHangman(int incorrectGuesses) {
    cout << hangmanDrawing[incorrectGuesses];
}
// Function to check if the guessed letter is in the secret word
bool checkGuess(const string& secretWord, char guess, string& guessedWord) {
    bool found = false;
    for (int i = 0; i < secretWord.length(); ++i) {
        if (secretWord[i] == guess) {
            guessedWord[i] = guess;
            found = true;
        }
    }
```

```
    return found;
}
int main() {
    // Initialize variables
    const string SECRET_WORD = "HANGMAN";
    const int MAX_INCORRECT_GUESSES = 6;
    int incorrectGuesses = 0;
    string guessedWord(SECRET_WORD.length(), '_');
    string guessedLetters = "";
    // Game loop
    while (incorrectGuesses < MAX_INCORRECT_GUESSES && guessedWord !=
SECRET_WORD) {
        // Display hangman graphics
        displayHangman(incorrectGuesses);
        // Display current state of the guessed word
        cout << "Guessed word: " << guessedWord << endl;
        // Display guessed letters
        cout << "Guessed letters: " << guessedLetters << endl;
        // Prompt the user for a guess
        char guess;
        cout << "Guess a letter: ";
        cin >> guess;
        // Check if the letter has already been guessed
        if (guessedLetters.find(guess) != string::npos) {
            cout << "You already guessed that letter. Try again." << endl;
            continue;
        }
        // Add the guessed letter to the list of guessed letters
        guessedLetters += guess;
        // Check if the guess is correct
        if (checkGuess(SECRET_WORD, guess, guessedWord)) {
            cout << "Correct guess!" << endl;
        } else {
            cout << "Incorrect guess!" << endl;
```

```
            incorrectGuesses++;
        }
    }
    // Display hangman graphics one final time
    displayHangman(incorrectGuesses);
    // Display the result
    if (guessedWord == SECRET_WORD) {
        cout << "Congratulations! You guessed the word: " << SECRET_WORD << endl;
    } else {
        cout << "Sorry, you've run out of guesses. The word was: " << SECRET_WORD << endl;
    }
    return 0;
}
```

30. Puzzle Slider Game

```
#include <iostream>
#include <vector>
#include <algorithm>
#include <ctime>
#include <cstdlib>
#include <conio.h>
using namespace std;
const int SIZE = 4; // Size of the puzzle (SIZE x SIZE)
const int EMPTY = 0; // Representation of the empty tile
// Function to initialize the puzzle board
vector<vector<int>> initializeBoard() {
    vector<vector<int>> board(SIZE, vector<int>(SIZE));
    int value = 1;
    for (int i = 0; i < SIZE; ++i) {
        for (int j = 0; j < SIZE; ++j) {
            board[i][j] = value;
            value++;
        }
    }
    board[SIZE - 1][SIZE - 1] = EMPTY; // Set the last tile as empty
    return board;
}
// Function to print the puzzle board
void printBoard(const vector<vector<int>>& board) {
    for (int i = 0; i < SIZE; ++i) {
        for (int j = 0; j < SIZE; ++j) {
            if (board[i][j] == EMPTY) {
                cout << "   "; // Print empty space
            } else {
                cout << board[i][j];
                if (board[i][j] < 10)
                    cout << "  "; // Add extra space for single-digit numbers
                else
                    cout << " "; // Add single space for double-digit numbers
```

```
            }
        }
        cout << endl;
    }
    cout << endl;
}
// Function to check if the puzzle is solved
bool isSolved(const vector<vector<int>>& board) {
    int value = 1;
    for (int i = 0; i < SIZE; ++i) {
        for (int j = 0; j < SIZE; ++j) {
            if (board[i][j] != value && !(i == SIZE - 1 && j == SIZE - 1))
                return false;
            value++;
        }
    }
    return true;
}
// Function to shuffle the puzzle board
void shuffleBoard(vector<vector<int>>& board, int moves) {
    srand(time(0));
    int dx[] = {0, 0, 1, -1};
    int dy[] = {1, -1, 0, 0};
    int emptyX = SIZE - 1;
    int emptyY = SIZE - 1;
    for (int i = 0; i < moves; ++i) {
        int randomMove = rand() % 4;
        int newX = emptyX + dx[randomMove];
        int newY = emptyY + dy[randomMove];
        if (newX >= 0 && newX < SIZE && newY >= 0 && newY < SIZE) {
            swap(board[emptyX][emptyY], board[newX][newY]);
            emptyX = newX;
            emptyY = newY;
        }
```

```
        }
    }
    // Function to get user input
    char getUserMove() {
        char move = getch();
        return move;
    }
    // Function to move the empty tile
    bool moveEmptyTile(vector<vector<int>>& board, char direction) {
        int dx = 0, dy = 0;
        switch (direction) {
            case 'w':
                dx = -1;
                break;
            case 's':
                dx = 1;
                break;
            case 'a':
                dy = -1;
                break;
            case 'd':
                dy = 1;
                break;
        }
        int emptyX, emptyY;
        // Find the position of the empty tile
        for (int i = 0; i < SIZE; ++i) {
            for (int j = 0; j < SIZE; ++j) {
                if (board[i][j] == EMPTY) {
                    emptyX = i;
                    emptyY = j;
                    break;
                }
            }
```

```
    }
    int newX = emptyX + dx;
    int newY = emptyY + dy;
    if (newX >= 0 && newX < SIZE && newY >= 0 && newY < SIZE) {
        swap(board[emptyX][emptyY], board[newX][newY]);
        return true;
    } else {
        return false;
    }
}
int main() {
    vector<vector<int>> puzzle = initializeBoard();
    shuffleBoard(puzzle, SIZE * SIZE * 10); // Shuffle the puzzle board
    cout << "Welcome to Puzzle Slider!" << endl;
    cout << "Use W, A, S, D to move the tiles and solve the puzzle." << endl;
    cout << "Press X to exit the game." << endl;
    printBoard(puzzle);
    while (!isSolved(puzzle)) {
        char move = getUserMove();
        if (move == 'x' || move == 'X') {
            cout << "Exiting the game..." << endl;
            break;
        } else if (move == 'w' || move == 's' || move == 'a' || move == 'd') {
            if (!moveEmptyTile(puzzle, move)) {
                cout << "Invalid move! Try again." << endl;
            }
            printBoard(puzzle);
        } else {
            cout << "Invalid input! Use W, A, S, D to move or X to exit." << endl;
        }
    }
    if (isSolved(puzzle)) {
        cout << "Congratulations! You solved the puzzle!" << endl;
    }   return 0;}
```

31. Jigsaw Puzzle Game

```
#include <iostream>
#include <vector>
#include <cstdlib>
#include <ctime>
#include <algorithm>
#include <iomanip>
using namespace std;
const int SIZE = 4; // Size of the puzzle (SIZE x SIZE)
const int EMPTY = 0; // Representation of the empty tile
// Function to initialize the puzzle board with shuffled pieces
vector<vector<int>> initializeBoard() {
    vector<vector<int>> board(SIZE, vector<int>(SIZE));
    int value = 1;
    for (int i = 0; i < SIZE; ++i) {
        for (int j = 0; j < SIZE; ++j) {
            board[i][j] = value;
            value++;
        }
    }
    board[SIZE - 1][SIZE - 1] = EMPTY; // Set the last tile as empty
    // Shuffle the puzzle pieces
    srand(time(0));
    for (int i = 0; i < SIZE * SIZE; ++i) {
        int x1 = rand() % SIZE;
        int y1 = rand() % SIZE;
        int x2 = rand() % SIZE;
        int y2 = rand() % SIZE;
        swap(board[x1][y1], board[x2][y2]);
    }
    return board;
}
// Function to print the puzzle board
void printBoard(const vector<vector<int>>& board) {
    for (int i = 0; i < SIZE; ++i) {
```

```
        for (int j = 0; j < SIZE; ++j) {
            if (board[i][j] == EMPTY) {
                cout << setw(3) << " "; // Print empty space
            } else {
                cout << setw(3) << board[i][j];
            }
        }
        cout << endl;
    }
    cout << endl;
}
// Function to check if the puzzle is solved
bool isSolved(const vector<vector<int>>& board) {
    int value = 1;
    for (int i = 0; i < SIZE; ++i) {
        for (int j = 0; j < SIZE; ++j) {
            if (board[i][j] != value && !(i == SIZE - 1 && j == SIZE - 1))
                return false;
            value++;
        }
    }
    return true;
}
// Function to get user input
char getUserMove() {
    char move;
    cout << "Enter move (W/A/S/D or X to exit): ";
    cin >> move;
    return move;
}
// Function to move a puzzle piece
bool movePiece(vector<vector<int>>& board, char direction) {
    int dx = 0, dy = 0;
    switch (direction) {
```

```
        case 'w':
          dx = -1;
          break;
        case 's':
          dx = 1;
          break;
        case 'a':
          dy = -1;
          break;
        case 'd':
          dy = 1;
          break;
        case 'x':
        case 'X':
          return false; // Exit the game
    }
    int emptyX, emptyY;
    // Find the position of the empty tile
    for (int i = 0; i < SIZE; ++i) {
        for (int j = 0; j < SIZE; ++j) {
            if (board[i][j] == EMPTY) {
                emptyX = i;
                emptyY = j;
                break;
            }
        }
    }
    int newX = emptyX + dx;
    int newY = emptyY + dy;
    if (newX >= 0 && newX < SIZE && newY >= 0 && newY < SIZE) {
        swap(board[emptyX][emptyY], board[newX][newY]);
        return true;
    } else {
        cout << "Invalid move! Try again." << endl;
```

```
        return false;
    }
}
int main() {
    vector<vector<int>> puzzle = initializeBoard();
    cout << "Welcome to Jigsaw Puzzle!" << endl;
    cout << "Use W, A, S, D to move puzzle pieces and solve the puzzle." << endl;
    cout << "Press X to exit the game." << endl;
    while (!isSolved(puzzle)) {
        printBoard(puzzle);
        char move = getUserMove();
        if (!movePiece(puzzle, move)) {
            break; // Exit the game if the user chooses to quit
        }
    }
    if (isSolved(puzzle)) {
        cout << "Congratulations! You solved the puzzle!" << endl;
    }
    return 0;
}
```

32. Sudoku Solver

```
#include <iostream>
using namespace std;
const int N = 9;
// Function to print the Sudoku grid
void printGrid(int grid[N][N]) {
   for (int row = 0; row < N; row++) {
      for (int col = 0; col < N; col++)
         cout << grid[row][col] << " ";
      cout << endl;
   }
}
// Function to check if a digit is safe to place at a given position
bool isSafe(int grid[N][N], int row, int col, int num) {
   // Check if the num is not already present in the current row
   for (int x = 0; x < N; x++)
      if (grid[row][x] == num)
         return false;
   // Check if the num is not already present in the current column
   for (int y = 0; y < N; y++)
      if (grid[y][col] == num)
         return false;
   // Check if the num is not already present in the current 3x3 subgrid
   int startRow = row - row % 3, startCol = col - col % 3;
   for (int i = 0; i < 3; i++)
      for (int j = 0; j < 3; j++)
         if (grid[i + startRow][j + startCol] == num)
            return false;
   return true;
}
// Function to solve the Sudoku puzzle using backtracking
bool solveSudoku(int grid[N][N]) {
   int row, col;
   // Find the first empty cell in the grid
   bool foundEmptyCell = false;
```

```
    for (row = 0; row < N; row++) {
        for (col = 0; col < N; col++) {
            if (grid[row][col] == 0) {
                foundEmptyCell = true;
                break;
            }
        }
        if (foundEmptyCell)
            break;
    }
    // If no empty cell is found, puzzle is solved
    if (!foundEmptyCell)
        return true;
    // Try placing digits from 1 to 9 in the empty cell
    for (int num = 1; num <= 9; num++) {
        // Check if it is safe to place num in the empty cell
        if (isSafe(grid, row, col, num)) {
            // Place num in the empty cell
            grid[row][col] = num;
            // Recursively solve the remaining puzzle
            if (solveSudoku(grid))
                return true;
            // If placing num doesn't lead to a solution, backtrack
            grid[row][col] = 0;
        }
    }
    // No solution found for the current configuration
    return false;
}
int main() {
    int grid[N][N] = {
        {5, 3, 0, 0, 7, 0, 0, 0, 0},
        {6, 0, 0, 1, 9, 5, 0, 0, 0},
        {0, 9, 8, 0, 0, 0, 0, 6, 0},
```

```
        {8, 0, 0, 0, 6, 0, 0, 0, 3},
        {4, 0, 0, 8, 0, 3, 0, 0, 1},
        {7, 0, 0, 0, 2, 0, 0, 0, 6},
        {0, 6, 0, 0, 0, 0, 2, 8, 0},
        {0, 0, 0, 4, 1, 9, 0, 0, 5},
        {0, 0, 0, 0, 8, 0, 0, 7, 9}
    };
    if (solveSudoku(grid))
        printGrid(grid);
    else
        cout << "No solution exists" << endl;
    return 0;
}
```

33. Shooting Gallery Game

```
#include <iostream>
#include <cstdlib>
#include <ctime>
using namespace std;
const int GALLERY_WIDTH = 10;
const int GALLERY_HEIGHT = 5;
const char TARGET_CHAR = 'T';
const char EMPTY_CHAR = '.';
const int NUM_TARGETS = 5;
const int MAX_SHOTS = 10;
// Function to initialize the gallery with targets randomly placed
void initializeGallery(char gallery[GALLERY_HEIGHT][GALLERY_WIDTH]) {
    for (int i = 0; i < GALLERY_HEIGHT; ++i) {
        for (int j = 0; j < GALLERY_WIDTH; ++j) {
            gallery[i][j] = EMPTY_CHAR;
        }
    }
    srand(time(0));
    for (int i = 0; i < NUM_TARGETS; ++i) {
        int x = rand() % GALLERY_WIDTH;
        int y = rand() % GALLERY_HEIGHT;
        gallery[y][x] = TARGET_CHAR;
    }
}
// Function to print the gallery
void printGallery(const char gallery[GALLERY_HEIGHT][GALLERY_WIDTH]) {
    for (int i = 0; i < GALLERY_HEIGHT; ++i) {
        for (int j = 0; j < GALLERY_WIDTH; ++j) {
            cout << gallery[i][j] << " ";
        }
        cout << endl;
    }
}
// Function to check if the player has hit a target
```

```
bool checkHit(char gallery[GALLERY_HEIGHT][GALLERY_WIDTH], int x, int y) {
    if (x >= 0 && x < GALLERY_WIDTH && y >= 0 && y < GALLERY_HEIGHT &&
gallery[y][x] == TARGET_CHAR) {
        gallery[y][x] = EMPTY_CHAR; // Remove the hit target
        return true;
    }
    return false;
}
int main() {
    char gallery[GALLERY_HEIGHT][GALLERY_WIDTH];
    int score = 0;
    int shotsFired = 0;
    initializeGallery(gallery);
    cout << "Welcome to the Shooting Gallery!" << endl;
    cout << "Hit as many targets as you can with " << MAX_SHOTS << " shots." << endl;
    cout << "Use the arrow keys to aim and press enter to shoot." << endl;
    while (shotsFired < MAX_SHOTS) {
        cout << "Score: " << score << "   Shots left: " << MAX_SHOTS - shotsFired << endl;
        printGallery(gallery);
        char input;
        cout << "Enter direction (u/d/l/r to aim, enter to shoot): ";
        cin >> input;
        int targetX = rand() % GALLERY_WIDTH;
        int targetY = rand() % GALLERY_HEIGHT;
        switch (input) {
            case 'u':
                targetY--;
                break;
            case 'd':
                targetY++;
                break;
            case 'l':
                targetX--;
                break;
```

```
            case 'r':
                targetX++;
                break;
            default:
                break;
        }
        if (checkHit(gallery, targetX, targetY)) {
            score++;
            cout << "Hit!" << endl;
        } else {
            cout << "Miss!" << endl;
        }
        shotsFired++;
    }
    cout << "Game over! Final score: " << score << endl;
    return 0;
}
```

34. Simon Says Game

```
#include <iostream>
#include <cstdlib>
#include <ctime>
#include <vector>
#include <chrono>
#include <thread>
using namespace std;
// Function to display a sequence of colors
void displaySequence(const vector<int>& sequence) {
    for (int color : sequence) {
        cout << color << " ";
        this_thread::sleep_for(chrono::milliseconds(500)); // Pause for 500 milliseconds between each
color
    }
    cout << endl;
}
// Function to generate a random sequence of colors
vector<int> generateSequence(int length) {
    vector<int> sequence;
    srand(time(0));
    for (int i = 0; i < length; ++i) {
        sequence.push_back(rand() % 4 + 1); // Randomly choose a color (1-4)
    }
    return sequence;
}
// Function to get user input for a color
int getUserInput() {
    int input;
    cout << "Enter your guess (1-4): ";
    cin >> input;
    return input;
}
// Function to check if the user's input matches the sequence
bool checkInput(const vector<int>& sequence, const vector<int>& userSequence) {
```

```
    if (sequence.size() != userSequence.size())
        return false;
    for (int i = 0; i < sequence.size(); ++i) {
        if (sequence[i] != userSequence[i])
            return false;
    }
    return true;
}
int main() {
    const int SEQUENCE_LENGTH = 5; // Length of the sequence
    vector<int> sequence = generateSequence(SEQUENCE_LENGTH);
    vector<int> userSequence;
    cout << "Welcome to Simon Says!" << endl;
    cout << "Watch the sequence of colors and repeat it." << endl;
    displaySequence(sequence);
    // Get user input
    for (int i = 0; i < SEQUENCE_LENGTH; ++i) {
        int input = getUserInput();
        userSequence.push_back(input);
    }
    // Check if the user's input matches the sequence
    if (checkInput(sequence, userSequence)) {
        cout << "Congratulations! You repeated the sequence correctly." << endl;
    } else {
        cout << "Sorry, you made a mistake. Game over!" << endl;
    }
    return 0;
}
```

35. Letter Guessing Game

```
#include <iostream>
#include <string>
#include <cstdlib>
#include <ctime>
#include <algorithm>
using namespace std;
// Function to randomly select a word from a list
string getRandomWord() {
    const int NUM_WORDS = 5;
    string words[NUM_WORDS] = {"apple", "banana", "orange", "grape", "kiwi"};
    srand(time(0));
    return words[rand() % NUM_WORDS];
}
// Function to check if the guessed letter is in the word
bool checkGuess(const string& word, char guess, string& guessedWord) {
    bool found = false;
    for (int i = 0; i < word.length(); ++i) {
        if (word[i] == guess) {
            guessedWord[i] = guess;
            found = true;
        }
    }
    return found;
}
int main() {
    string word = getRandomWord();
    string guessedWord(word.length(), '_');
    int attempts = 5;
    cout << "Welcome to the Letter Guessing Game!" << endl;
    cout << "Try to guess the word by guessing one letter at a time." << endl;
    cout << "You have " << attempts << " attempts." << endl;

    while (attempts > 0 && guessedWord != word) {
        cout << "Current guessed word: " << guessedWord << endl;
```

```
        char guess;
        cout << "Enter a letter guess: ";
        cin >> guess;
        if (checkGuess(word, guess, guessedWord)) {
            cout << "Correct guess!" << endl;
        } else {
            cout << "Incorrect guess!" << endl;
            attempts--;
            cout << "Attempts left: " << attempts << endl;
        }
    }
    if (guessedWord == word) {
        cout << "Congratulations! You guessed the word: " << word << endl;
    } else {
        cout << "Sorry, you ran out of attempts. The word was: " << word << endl;
    }
    return 0;
}
```

36. Basketball Shooting Game

```
#include <iostream>
#include <cstdlib>
#include <ctime>
using namespace std;
// Function to simulate shooting a basketball
bool shootBasketball() {
    // Simulate the chance of making a shot (50% chance)
    return rand() % 2 == 0;
}
int main() {
    srand(time(0));
    int score = 0;
    int attempts = 10;
    cout << "Welcome to the Basketball Shooting Game!" << endl;
    cout << "You have " << attempts << " attempts to score as many points as possible." << endl;
    for (int i = 0; i < attempts; ++i) {
        cout << "Attempt " << i + 1 << ": ";
        if (shootBasketball()) {
            cout << "You made the shot! +1 point" << endl;
            score++;
        } else {
            cout << "You missed the shot." << endl;
        }
    }
    cout << "Game over!" << endl;
    cout << "Your final score: " << score << " points" << endl;
    return 0;
}
```

37. Simple Physics Simulation

```
#include <iostream>
#include <cmath>
using namespace std;
const double GRAVITY = 9.81; // Acceleration due to gravity in m/s^2
// Function to calculate the horizontal distance traveled by a projectile
double horizontalDistance(double initialVelocity, double angle, double time) {
    return initialVelocity * cos(angle) * time;
}
// Function to calculate the vertical distance traveled by a projectile
double verticalDistance(double initialVelocity, double angle, double time) {
    return initialVelocity * sin(angle) * time - 0.5 * GRAVITY * time * time;
}
int main() {
    double initialVelocity, angle;
    cout << "Enter the initial velocity (m/s): ";
    cin >> initialVelocity;
    cout << "Enter the launch angle (degrees): ";
    cin >> angle;
    angle *= M_PI / 180.0; // Convert angle from degrees to radians
    double maxHeight = (initialVelocity * initialVelocity * sin(angle) * sin(angle)) / (2 *
GRAVITY);
    double totalTime = (2 * initialVelocity * sin(angle)) / GRAVITY;
    double maxHorizontalDistance = horizontalDistance(initialVelocity, angle, totalTime);
    cout << "Maximum height reached: " << maxHeight << " meters" << endl;
    cout << "Total time of flight: " << totalTime << " seconds" << endl;
    cout << "Maximum horizontal distance: " << maxHorizontalDistance << " meters" << endl;
    return 0;
}
```

38. Leap Year Checker Game

```
#include <iostream>
using namespace std;
// Function to check if a year is a leap year
bool isLeapYear(int year) {
   // A year is a leap year if it is divisible by 4,
   // but not divisible by 100, except if it is also divisible by 400
   if ((year % 4 == 0 && year % 100 != 0) || (year % 400 == 0))
      return true;
   else
      return false;
}
int main() {
   int year;
   cout << "Enter a year: ";
   cin >> year;
   if (isLeapYear(year))
      cout << year << " is a leap year." << endl;
   else
      cout << year << " is not a leap year." << endl;
   return 0;
}
```

39. Virtual Pet Simulation

```
#include <iostream>
#include <string>
#include <ctime>
#include <cstdlib>
using namespace std;
class VirtualPet {
private:
    string name;
    int hunger;
    int happiness;
public:
    // Constructor
    VirtualPet(string petName) : name(petName), hunger(50), happiness(50) {}

    // Function to feed the pet
    void feed() {
        hunger -= 10;
        if (hunger < 0)
            hunger = 0;
    }
    // Function to play with the pet
    void play() {
        happiness += 10;
        if (happiness > 100)
            happiness = 100;
    }
    // Function to check if the pet is alive
    bool isAlive() {
        return (hunger > 0 && happiness > 0);
    }
    // Function to display pet status
    void displayStatus() {
        cout << "Name: " << name << endl;
        cout << "Hunger: " << hunger << endl;
```

```
        cout << "Happiness: " << happiness << endl;
    }
};
int main() {
    srand(time(0));
    cout << "Welcome to Virtual Pet Simulation!" << endl;
    cout << "Enter a name for your pet: ";
    string petName;
    cin >> petName;
    VirtualPet pet(petName);
    while (pet.isAlive()) {
        pet.displayStatus();
        cout << "Options:" << endl;
        cout << "1. Feed the pet" << endl;
        cout << "2. Play with the pet" << endl;
        cout << "3. Do nothing" << endl;
        int choice;
        cout << "Enter your choice: ";
        cin >> choice;
        switch (choice) {
            case 1:
                pet.feed();
                cout << "You feed " << petName << "." << endl;
                break;
            case 2:
                pet.play();
                cout << "You play with " << petName << "." << endl;
                break;
```

```
            case 3:
                cout << "You do nothing." << endl;
                break;
            default:
                cout << "Invalid choice!" << endl;
        }
        // Simulate passage of time
        pet.feed();
        pet.play();
    }
    cout << petName << " has passed away. Game over!" << endl;
    return 0;
}
```

40. Maze Generator and Solver

```
#include <iostream>
#include <vector>
#include <stack>
#include <ctime>
#include <cstdlib>
using namespace std;
// Maze dimensions
const int ROWS = 10;
const int COLS = 10;
// Cell states
const char EMPTY_CELL = ' ';
const char WALL_CELL = '#';
const char VISITED_CELL = '.';
const char PATH_CELL = 'X';
// Directions: Up, Right, Down, Left
const int DX[] = {-1, 0, 1, 0};
const int DY[] = {0, 1, 0, -1};
// Cell structure to represent a cell in the maze
struct Cell {
   int row, col;
   bool visited;
   vector<int> walls;
   Cell(int r, int c) : row(r), col(c), visited(false) {
      walls = {1, 1, 1, 1}; // Each wall initially exists
   }
};
// Function to generate the maze using Depth-First Search algorithm
void generateMaze(vector<vector<Cell>>& maze, int startRow, int startCol) {
   stack<Cell*> cellStack;
   Cell* currentCell = &maze[startRow][startCol];
   currentCell->visited = true;
   cellStack.push(currentCell);
   while (!cellStack.empty()) {
      currentCell = cellStack.top();
```

```
        int row = currentCell->row;
        int col = currentCell->col;
        // Find unvisited neighbor cells
        vector<int> unvisitedNeighbors;
        for (int i = 0; i < 4; ++i) {
            int newRow = row + DX[i];
            int newCol = col + DY[i];
            if (newRow >= 0 && newRow < ROWS && newCol >= 0 && newCol < COLS &&
!maze[newRow][newCol].visited)
                unvisitedNeighbors.push_back(i);
        }
        if (!unvisitedNeighbors.empty()) {
            int randIndex = rand() % unvisitedNeighbors.size();
            int direction = unvisitedNeighbors[randIndex];
            int newRow = row + DX[direction];
            int newCol = col + DY[direction];
            // Remove the wall between current cell and the chosen neighbor cell
            maze[row][col].walls[direction] = 0;
            maze[newRow][newCol].walls[(direction + 2) % 4] = 0;

            // Mark the neighbor cell as visited and push it to the stack
            maze[newRow][newCol].visited = true;
            cellStack.push(&maze[newRow][newCol]);
        } else {
            cellStack.pop();
        }
    }
}
// Function to initialize the maze grid
vector<vector<Cell>> initializeMaze() {
    vector<vector<Cell>> maze(ROWS, vector<Cell>(COLS, Cell(0, 0)));
    return maze;
}
// Function to print the maze
```

```
void printMaze(const vector<vector<Cell>>& maze) {
    for (int i = 0; i < ROWS; ++i) {
        for (int j = 0; j < COLS; ++j) {
            cout << (maze[i][j].walls[0] ? WALL_CELL : EMPTY_CELL) << WALL_CELL;
        }
        cout << endl;
        for (int j = 0; j < COLS; ++j) {
            cout << (maze[i][j].walls[3] ? WALL_CELL : EMPTY_CELL) << (maze[i][j].visited ?
VISITED_CELL : EMPTY_CELL);
        }
        cout << (maze[i][COLS - 1].walls[1] ? WALL_CELL : EMPTY_CELL) << endl;
    }
    for (int j = 0; j < COLS; ++j) {
        cout << WALL_CELL << (maze[ROWS - 1][j].walls[2] ? WALL_CELL : EMPTY_CELL);
    }
    cout << WALL_CELL << endl;
}
int main() {
    srand(time(0));
    vector<vector<Cell>> maze = initializeMaze();
    int startRow = rand() % ROWS;
    int startCol = rand() % COLS;
    generateMaze(maze, startRow, startCol);
    printMaze(maze);
    return 0;
}
```

41. Math Quiz Game

```
#include <iostream>
#include <ctime>
#include <cstdlib>
using namespace std;
// Function to generate a random number between min and max (inclusive)
int getRandomNumber(int min, int max) {
  return rand() % (max - min + 1) + min;
}
// Function to generate a math question
void generateQuestion() {
  int num1 = getRandomNumber(1, 10);
  int num2 = getRandomNumber(1, 10);
  char operators[] = {'+', '-', '*', '/'};
  char op = operators[getRandomNumber(0, 3)];
  // Display the question
  cout << "What is " << num1 << " " << op << " " << num2 << "? ";
  // Get user input
  int answer;
  cin >> answer;
  // Calculate the correct answer
  int correctAnswer;
  switch (op) {
    case '+':
      correctAnswer = num1 + num2;
      break;
    case '-':
      correctAnswer = num1 - num2;
      break;
    case '*':
      correctAnswer = num1 * num2;
      break;
    case '/':
      correctAnswer = num1 / num2;
```

```
            break;
    }
    // Check the answer
    if (answer == correctAnswer) {
        cout << "Correct!" << endl;
    } else {
        cout << "Incorrect. The correct answer is " << correctAnswer << endl;
    }
}
int main() {
    srand(time(0));
    cout << "Welcome to the Math Quiz Game!" << endl;
    cout << "You will be asked to solve simple math problems." << endl;
    cout << "Let's begin!" << endl;
    int numQuestions;
    cout << "How many questions would you like to answer? ";
    cin >> numQuestions;
    for (int i = 0; i < numQuestions; ++i) {
        cout << "Question " << i + 1 << ": ";
        generateQuestion();
    }
    cout << "Thank you for playing!" << endl;
    return 0;
}
```

42. Lunar Lander Game

```
#include <iostream>
#include <cstdlib>
#include <ctime>
#include <cmath>
using namespace std;
// Constants
const double GRAVITY = 1.622; // Gravity on the moon's surface (m/s^2)
const double FUEL_CONSUMPTION_RATE = 0.1; // Fuel consumption rate per second (units/s)
const double MAX_FUEL = 100; // Maximum fuel capacity
const double MAX_VELOCITY = 10; // Maximum landing velocity allowed (m/s)
const double SAFE_LANDING_SPEED = 2; // Safe landing speed (m/s)
// Function to calculate the velocity of the lander
double calculateVelocity(double fuel, double acceleration, double time) {
   // Using the formula: velocity = initial_velocity + acceleration * time
   return GRAVITY * time - FUEL_CONSUMPTION_RATE * fuel;
}
// Function to display the status of the lander
void displayStatus(double altitude, double velocity, double fuel) {
   cout << "Altitude: " << altitude << " m" << endl;
   cout << "Velocity: " << velocity << " m/s" << endl;
   cout << "Fuel: " << fuel << " units" << endl;
}
int main() {
   srand(time(0));
   double altitude = 1000; // Initial altitude (m)
   double velocity = 0; // Initial velocity (m/s)
   double fuel = MAX_FUEL; // Initial fuel level (units)
   cout << "Welcome to Lunar Lander!" << endl;
   cout << "Your goal is to land the lunar lander safely on the moon's surface." << endl;
   cout << "You have a limited amount of fuel to control the descent." << endl;

   while (altitude > 0) {
      displayStatus(altitude, velocity, fuel);
      double throttle;
```

```
        cout << "Enter throttle (0-100): ";
        cin >> throttle;
        // Clamp throttle value between 0 and 100
        throttle = max(0.0, min(100.0, throttle));
        // Calculate acceleration based on throttle and fuel consumption
        double acceleration = GRAVITY - FUEL_CONSUMPTION_RATE * throttle / MAX_FUEL;
        // Update velocity and altitude
        velocity = calculateVelocity(fuel, acceleration, 1);
        altitude -= velocity;
        // Consume fuel
        fuel -= FUEL_CONSUMPTION_RATE * throttle;
        // Check for landing conditions
        if (altitude <= 0) {
          if (abs(velocity) <= SAFE_LANDING_SPEED) {
            cout << "Safe landing! Congratulations!" << endl;
          } else {
            cout << "Landing failed! The lander crashed." << endl;
          }
        } else if (fuel <= 0) {
          cout << "Out of fuel! The lander crashed." << endl;
          break;
        } else if (abs(velocity) > MAX_VELOCITY) {
          cout << "Exceeded maximum landing velocity! The lander crashed." << endl;
          break;
        }
      }
      return 0;}
```

43. Target Shooting Game

```
#include <iostream>
#include <cstdlib>
#include <ctime>
#include <cmath>
using namespace std;
// Constants
const int TARGET_RADIUS = 5; // Radius of the target
const int TARGET_CENTER_X = 50; // X-coordinate of the target center
const int TARGET_CENTER_Y = 50; // Y-coordinate of the target center
const int MAX_ATTEMPTS = 5; // Maximum number of attempts
// Function to calculate the distance between two points
double calculateDistance(int x1, int y1, int x2, int y2) {
  return sqrt(pow(x2 - x1, 2) + pow(y2 - y1, 2));
}
int main() {
  srand(time(0));
  cout << "Welcome to Target Shooting Game!" << endl;
  cout << "Hit the target at (" << TARGET_CENTER_X << ", " << TARGET_CENTER_Y << ")
with a radius of " << TARGET_RADIUS << "." << endl;
  cout << "You have " << MAX_ATTEMPTS << " attempts." << endl;
  int numAttempts = 0;
  while (numAttempts < MAX_ATTEMPTS) {
    int x, y;
    cout << "Enter coordinates (x y) to shoot: ";
    cin >> x >> y;
    // Calculate the distance from the shot to the target center
    double distance = calculateDistance(x, y, TARGET_CENTER_X, TARGET_CENTER_Y);
    // Check if the shot hits the target
    if (distance <= TARGET_RADIUS) {
      cout << "Congratulations! You hit the target!" << endl;
      break;
    } else {
      cout << "Miss! Try again." << endl;
    }
```

```
        numAttempts++;
    }
    if (numAttempts == MAX_ATTEMPTS) {
        cout << "You have run out of attempts. Game over." << endl;
    }
    return 0;
}
```

44. Weather Simulation Game

```
#include <iostream>
#include <cstdlib>
#include <ctime>
using namespace std;
// Enum to represent weather conditions
enum Weather {
    SUNNY,
    CLOUDY,
    RAINY,
    SNOWY
};
// Function to generate random weather
Weather generateWeather() {
    int weatherIndex = rand() % 4;
    return static_cast<Weather>(weatherIndex);
}
// Function to convert weather enum to string
string weatherToString(Weather weather) {
    switch (weather) {
        case SUNNY:
            return "Sunny";
        case CLOUDY:
            return "Cloudy";
        case RAINY:
            return "Rainy";
        case SNOWY:
            return "Snowy";
        default:
            return "Unknown";
    }
}
int main() {
    srand(time(0));
    cout << "Welcome to Weather Simulation Game!" << endl;
```

```
    cout << "Predict the weather for tomorrow." << endl;
    Weather actualWeather = generateWeather();
    int prediction;
    cout << "Enter your prediction (0 = Sunny, 1 = Cloudy, 2 = Rainy, 3 = Snowy): ";
    cin >> prediction;
    Weather predictedWeather = static_cast<Weather>(prediction);
    cout << "Actual Weather: " << weatherToString(actualWeather) << endl;
    cout << "Your Prediction: " << weatherToString(predictedWeather) << endl;
    if (actualWeather == predictedWeather) {
        cout << "Congratulations! Your prediction was correct!" << endl;
    } else {
        cout << "Sorry, your prediction was incorrect." << endl;
    }
    return 0;
}
```

45. Simple Music Player Game

```
#include <iostream>
#include <vector>
#include <ctime>
#include <cstdlib>
using namespace std;
// Define a structure for a song
struct Song {
    string title;
    string artist;
    int duration; // in seconds
    // Constructor
    Song(string t, string a, int d) : title(t), artist(a), duration(d) {}
};
// Function to display the menu
void displayMenu() {
    cout << "Music Player" << endl;
    cout << "1. Play a random song" << endl;
    cout << "2. Exit" << endl;
    cout << "Enter your choice: ";
}
// Function to play a random song
void playRandomSong(const vector<Song>& songs) {
    if (songs.empty()) {
        cout << "No songs available." << endl;
        return;
    }
    int randomIndex = rand() % songs.size();
    const Song& song = songs[randomIndex];
    cout << "Now playing: " << song.title << " by " << song.artist << " (" << song.duration << "
seconds)" << endl;
}
int main() {
    srand(time(0));
    // Create some sample songs
```

```
    vector<Song> songs;
    songs.push_back(Song("Song 1", "Artist 1", 180));
    songs.push_back(Song("Song 2", "Artist 2", 240));
    songs.push_back(Song("Song 3", "Artist 3", 200));
    int choice;
    do {
        displayMenu();
        cin >> choice;
        switch (choice) {
            case 1:
                playRandomSong(songs);
                break;
            case 2:
                cout << "Exiting..." << endl;
                break;
            default:
                cout << "Invalid choice. Please try again." << endl;
        }
    } while (choice != 2);
    return 0;
}
```

46. Word Scramble Game

```
#include <iostream>
#include <string>
#include <vector>
#include <cstdlib>
#include <ctime>
#include <algorithm>
using namespace std;
// Function to scramble a word
string scrambleWord(const string& word) {
    string scrambledWord = word;
    random_shuffle(scrambledWord.begin(), scrambledWord.end());
    return scrambledWord;
}
// Function to check if a word is valid (contained in the word list)
bool isValidWord(const string& word, const vector<string>& wordList) {
    return find(wordList.begin(), wordList.end(), word) != wordList.end();
}
int main() {
    srand(time(0));
    // List of words
    vector<string> wordList = {"hello", "world", "apple", "banana", "computer"};
    // Select a random word from the list
    string targetWord = wordList[rand() % wordList.size()];
    // Scramble the word
    string scrambledWord = scrambleWord(targetWord);
    cout << "Welcome to Word Scramble Game!" << endl;
    cout << "Unscramble the word: " << scrambledWord << endl;
    string guess;
    do {
        cout << "Enter your guess (or 'quit' to quit): ";
        cin >> guess;
        if (guess == "quit") {
            cout << "The word was: " << targetWord << endl;
            break;
```

```
        }
        if (guess == targetWord) {
            cout << "Congratulations! You guessed it correctly!" << endl;
            break;
        } else {
            cout << "Incorrect guess. Try again." << endl;
        }
    } while (true);
    return 0;
}
```

47. Reaction Time Game with Colors

```
#include <iostream>
#include <ctime>
#include <cstdlib>
#include <chrono>
#include <thread>
using namespace std;
// Function to generate a random color
string generateColor() {
    string colors[] = {"Red", "Green", "Blue", "Yellow", "Purple", "Orange"};
    return colors[rand() % 6];
}
int main() {
    srand(time(0));
    cout << "Welcome to Reaction Time Game with Colors!" << endl;
    cout << "You will see a color name printed on the screen." << endl;
    cout << "Press Enter as quickly as possible when the color matches the name." << endl;
    cout << "Let's start!" << endl;
    while (true) {
        // Generate a random color
        string color = generateColor();
        // Print the color name
        cout << "Color: " << color << endl;
        // Record the start time
        auto startTime = chrono::steady_clock::now();
        // Wait for user input
        string input;
        getline(cin, input);
        // Record the end time
        auto endTime = chrono::steady_clock::now();
        // Calculate reaction time in milliseconds
        auto reactionTime = chrono::duration_cast<chrono::milliseconds>(endTime -
startTime).count();
        // Display reaction time
        cout << "Reaction Time: " << reactionTime << " milliseconds" << endl;
```

```
        // Pause for a moment before the next round
        this_thread::sleep_for(chrono::seconds(1));
      // Clear the screen for the next round
        cout << "\033[2J\033[1;1H"; // ANSI escape sequence to clear the screen
    }
    return 0;
}
```

48. Simple Slot Machine

```
#include <iostream>
#include <cstdlib>
#include <ctime>
using namespace std;
// Function to generate a random number between min and max (inclusive)
int getRandomNumber(int min, int max) {
   return rand() % (max - min + 1) + min;
}
int main() {
   srand(time(0));
   cout << "Welcome to the Slot Machine Game!" << endl;
   cout << "Match three numbers to win!" << endl;
   while (true) {
      cout << "Press Enter to spin the wheels...";
      cin.ignore(); // Wait for user to press Enter
      system("cls"); // Clear the screen (for Windows, use "cls"; for Linux/macOS, use "clear")
      // Generate random numbers for the wheels
      int wheel1 = getRandomNumber(1, 9);
      int wheel2 = getRandomNumber(1, 9);
      int wheel3 = getRandomNumber(1, 9);
      // Display the numbers on the wheels
      cout << "Wheels: " << wheel1 << " " << wheel2 << " " << wheel3 << endl;
      // Check if all numbers match
      if (wheel1 == wheel2 && wheel2 == wheel3) {
         cout << "Congratulations! You win!" << endl;
      } else {
         cout << "Sorry, try again." << endl;
      }
   }
   return 0;
}
```

49. Building Blocks Tower Game

```
#include <iostream>
#include <cstdlib>
#include <ctime>
using namespace std;
const int MAX_HEIGHT = 10; // Maximum height of the tower
// Function to display the tower
void displayTower(int height) {
   for (int i = 0; i < height; ++i) {
      for (int j = 0; j < height - i - 1; ++j) {
         cout << " ";
      }
      for (int j = 0; j < 2 * i + 1; ++j) {
         cout << "*";
      }
      cout << endl;
   }
}
int main() {
   srand(time(0));
   cout << "Welcome to the Building Blocks Tower Game!" << endl;
   cout << "Build the tallest tower you can!" << endl;
   int currentHeight = 1; // Current height of the tower
   while (true) {
      // Display the tower
      cout << "Tower Height: " << currentHeight << endl;
      displayTower(currentHeight);
      // Prompt the user to continue or stop
      cout << "Press Enter to add a block or type 'quit' to stop: ";
      string input;
      getline(cin, input);
      if (input == "quit") {
         cout << "Thanks for playing! Your final tower height is: " << currentHeight << endl;
         break;
      }
```

```
        // Add a block to the tower
        if (currentHeight < MAX_HEIGHT) {
            currentHeight++;
        } else {
            cout << "Maximum height reached!" << endl;
        }
        // Clear the screen
        system("cls"); // For Windows. For Linux/macOS, use "clear"
    }
    return 0;
}
```

50. Pac-Man Style Maze Game

```
#include <SFML/Graphics.hpp>
int main() {
    sf::RenderWindow window(sf::VideoMode(800, 600), "Pac-Man Style Maze Game");
    // Load Pac-Man texture
    sf::Texture pacmanTexture;
    if (!pacmanTexture.loadFromFile("pacman.png")) {
        return EXIT_FAILURE;
    }
    // Set up Pac-Man sprite
    sf::Sprite pacman(pacmanTexture);
    pacman.setScale(0.1f, 0.1f);
    pacman.setPosition(400, 300);
    // Main game loop
    while (window.isOpen()) {
        sf::Event event;
        while (window.pollEvent(event)) {
            if (event.type == sf::Event::Closed) {
                window.close();
            }
        }
        // Handle user input for Pac-Man movement
        if (sf::Keyboard::isKeyPressed(sf::Keyboard::Up)) {
            pacman.move(0, -5);
        }
        if (sf::Keyboard::isKeyPressed(sf::Keyboard::Down)) {
            pacman.move(0, 5);
        }
        if (sf::Keyboard::isKeyPressed(sf::Keyboard::Left)) {
            pacman.move(-5, 0);
        }
        if (sf::Keyboard::isKeyPressed(sf::Keyboard::Right)) {
            pacman.move(5, 0);
        }
        window.clear();
```

```
        window.draw(pacman);
        window.display();
    }
    return 0;
}
```

51. Breakout with Power-ups

```
#include <SFML/Graphics.hpp>
#include <iostream>
#include <cstdlib>
#include <ctime>
using namespace std;
const int SCREEN_WIDTH = 800;
const int SCREEN_HEIGHT = 600;
const int PADDLE_WIDTH = 100;
const int PADDLE_HEIGHT = 20;
const int PADDLE_SPEED = 6;
const int BALL_RADIUS = 10;
const int BALL_SPEED = 5;
const int BRICK_WIDTH = 60;
const int BRICK_HEIGHT = 20;
const int NUM_ROWS = 5;
const int NUM_COLS = 10;
enum class PowerUpType {
    None,
    LongerPaddle,
    FasterBall
};
struct Brick {
    sf::RectangleShape shape;
    bool destroyed;
};
sf::RectangleShape createPaddle() {
    sf::RectangleShape paddle(sf::Vector2f(PADDLE_WIDTH, PADDLE_HEIGHT));
    paddle.setFillColor(sf::Color::Green);
    paddle.setPosition((SCREEN_WIDTH - PADDLE_WIDTH) / 2, SCREEN_HEIGHT -
PADDLE_HEIGHT - 10);
    return paddle;
}
sf::CircleShape createBall() {
    sf::CircleShape ball(BALL_RADIUS);
```

```
    ball.setFillColor(sf::Color::Yellow);
    ball.setPosition((SCREEN_WIDTH - BALL_RADIUS) / 2, SCREEN_HEIGHT -
PADDLE_HEIGHT - BALL_RADIUS - 20);
    return ball;
}
void movePaddle(sf::RectangleShape& paddle) {
    if (sf::Keyboard::isKeyPressed(sf::Keyboard::Left) && paddle.getPosition().x > 0) {
        paddle.move(-PADDLE_SPEED, 0);
    }
    if (sf::Keyboard::isKeyPressed(sf::Keyboard::Right) && paddle.getPosition().x +
PADDLE_WIDTH < SCREEN_WIDTH) {
        paddle.move(PADDLE_SPEED, 0);
    }
}
void moveBall(sf::CircleShape& ball, sf::Vector2f& ballVelocity) {
    ball.move(ballVelocity);
    if (ball.getPosition().x < 0 || ball.getPosition().x > SCREEN_WIDTH - BALL_RADIUS) {
        ballVelocity.x = -ballVelocity.x;
    }
    if (ball.getPosition().y < 0 || ball.getPosition().y > SCREEN_HEIGHT - BALL_RADIUS) {
        ballVelocity.y = -ballVelocity.y;
    }
}
bool isColliding(const sf::RectangleShape& brick, const sf::CircleShape& ball) {
    sf::FloatRect brickBounds = brick.getGlobalBounds();
    sf::FloatRect ballBounds = ball.getGlobalBounds();
    return brickBounds.intersects(ballBounds);
}
PowerUpType generatePowerUp() {
    int randNum = rand() % 10;
    if (randNum < 2) return PowerUpType::LongerPaddle;
    else if (randNum < 4) return PowerUpType::FasterBall;
    else return PowerUpType::None;
}
```

```
int main() {
   srand(time(0));
   sf::RenderWindow window(sf::VideoMode(SCREEN_WIDTH, SCREEN_HEIGHT), "Breakout
with Power-ups");
   sf::RectangleShape paddle = createPaddle();
   sf::CircleShape ball = createBall();
   sf::Vector2f ballVelocity(BALL_SPEED, -BALL_SPEED);
   vector<Brick> bricks;
   for (int i = 0; i < NUM_ROWS; ++i) {
      for (int j = 0; j < NUM_COLS; ++j) {
         Brick brick;
         brick.shape.setSize(sf::Vector2f(BRICK_WIDTH, BRICK_HEIGHT));
         brick.shape.setFillColor(sf::Color::Blue);
         brick.shape.setPosition(j * (BRICK_WIDTH + 2) + 2, i * (BRICK_HEIGHT + 2) + 2);
         brick.destroyed = false;
         bricks.push_back(brick);
      }
   }
   PowerUpType activePowerUp = PowerUpType::None;
   sf::Clock powerUpTimer;
   while (window.isOpen()) {
      sf::Event event;
      while (window.pollEvent(event)) {
         if (event.type == sf::Event::Closed) {
            window.close();
         }
      }
      movePaddle(paddle);
      moveBall(ball, ballVelocity);
      for (auto& brick : bricks) {
         if (!brick.destroyed && isColliding(brick.shape, ball)) {
            brick.destroyed = true;
            ballVelocity.y = -ballVelocity.y;
            PowerUpType newPowerUp = generatePowerUp();
```

```
            if (newPowerUp != PowerUpType::None) {
                activePowerUp = newPowerUp;
                powerUpTimer.restart();
            }
            break;
        }
    }
    if (isColliding(paddle, ball)) {
        ballVelocity.y = -ballVelocity.y;
    }
    if (activePowerUp != PowerUpType::None && powerUpTimer.getElapsedTime().asSeconds() >=
10) {
        activePowerUp = PowerUpType::None;
    }
    window.clear();
    for (auto& brick : bricks) {
        if (!brick.destroyed) {
            window.draw(brick.shape);
        }
    }
    window.draw(paddle);
    window.draw(ball);
    window.display();
}
return 0; }
```

52. Fishing Game

```
#include <iostream>
#include <cstdlib>
#include <ctime>
#include <string>
using namespace std;
// Function to generate a random fish
string generateFish() {
    string fish[] = {"Carp", "Trout", "Salmon", "Bass", "Perch"};
    return fish[rand() % 5];
}
int main() {
    srand(time(0));
    cout << "Welcome to the Fishing Game!" << endl;
    cout << "Try to catch some fish!" << endl;
    int numFishCaught = 0;
    while (true) {
        cout << "Press Enter to cast your line...";
        cin.ignore(); // Wait for user to press Enter
        // Generate a random fish
        string caughtFish = generateFish();
        // Check if a fish was caught
        if (caughtFish != "No fish") {
            cout << "You caught a " << caughtFish << "!" << endl;
            numFishCaught++;
        } else {
            cout << "No fish caught this time." << endl;
        }
        // Check if player wants to continue fishing
        cout << "Would you like to fish again? (yes/no): ";
        string choice;
        cin >> choice;
        if (choice == "no") {
            break;
        }
```

```
    }
    cout << "Thanks for playing! You caught " << numFishCaught << " fish." << endl;
    return 0;
}
```

53. Minesweeper Game

```
#include <iostream>
#include <vector>
#include <cstdlib>
#include <ctime>
#include <iomanip>
using namespace std;
const int BOARD_SIZE = 10;
const int NUM_MINES = 10;
// Function to initialize the board with mines
void initializeBoard(vector<vector<char>>& board) {
    for (int i = 0; i < BOARD_SIZE; ++i) {
        for (int j = 0; j < BOARD_SIZE; ++j) {
            board[i][j] = '-';
        }
    }
    int minesPlaced = 0;
    while (minesPlaced < NUM_MINES) {
        int x = rand() % BOARD_SIZE;
        int y = rand() % BOARD_SIZE;
        if (board[x][y] != '*') {
            board[x][y] = '*';
            minesPlaced++;
        }
    }
}
// Function to display the board
void displayBoard(const vector<vector<char>>& board, bool showMines = false) {
    cout << "  ";
    for (int i = 0; i < BOARD_SIZE; ++i) {
        cout << setw(2) << i;
    }
    cout << endl;
    for (int i = 0; i < BOARD_SIZE; ++i) {
        cout << setw(2) << i;
```

```
        for (int j = 0; j < BOARD_SIZE; ++j) {
            if (board[i][j] == '*' && !showMines) {
                cout << setw(2) << '-';
            } else {
                cout << setw(2) << board[i][j];
            }
        }
        cout << endl;
    }
}
// Function to count the number of adjacent mines
int countAdjacentMines(const vector<vector<char>>& board, int row, int col) {
    int count = 0;
    for (int i = -1; i <= 1; ++i) {
        for (int j = -1; j <= 1; ++j) {
            int newRow = row + i;
            int newCol = col + j;
            if (newRow >= 0 && newRow < BOARD_SIZE && newCol >= 0 && newCol <
BOARD_SIZE && board[newRow][newCol] == '*') {
                count++;
            }
        }
    }
    return count;
}
// Function to reveal the cell and recursively reveal adjacent cells
void revealCell(vector<vector<char>>& board, vector<vector<bool>>& visited, int row, int col) {
    if (row < 0 || row >= BOARD_SIZE || col < 0 || col >= BOARD_SIZE || visited[row][col]) {
        return;
    }
    visited[row][col] = true;
    if (board[row][col] != '-') {
        return;
    }
```

```
    int numMines = countAdjacentMines(board, row, col);
    board[row][col] = numMines == 0 ? ' ' : numMines + '0';
    if (numMines == 0) {
        for (int i = -1; i <= 1; ++i) {
            for (int j = -1; j <= 1; ++j) {
                revealCell(board, visited, row + i, col + j);
            }
        }
    }
}
int main() {
    srand(time(0));
    vector<vector<char>> board(BOARD_SIZE, vector<char>(BOARD_SIZE));
    vector<vector<bool>> visited(BOARD_SIZE, vector<bool>(BOARD_SIZE, false));
    initializeBoard(board);
    cout << "Welcome to Minesweeper!" << endl;
    cout << "Rules: Uncover all cells without detonating any mines." << endl;
    cout << "Enter row and column coordinates to uncover a cell." << endl;
    cout << "To uncover a cell, enter coordinates separated by a space (e.g., '3 5')." << endl;
    bool gameWon = false;
    int cellsUncovered = 0;
    while (!gameWon) {
        displayBoard(board);
        int row, col;
        cout << "Enter row and column coordinates: ";
        cin >> row >> col;
        if (row < 0 || row >= BOARD_SIZE || col < 0 || col >= BOARD_SIZE || visited[row][col]) {
            cout << "Invalid input. Try again." << endl;
            continue;
        }
        if (board[row][col] == '*') {
            cout << "Game over! You detonated a mine." << endl;
            displayBoard(board, true); // Show mines
            break;
```

```
        }
        revealCell(board, visited, row, col);
        cellsUncovered++;
        if (cellsUncovered == BOARD_SIZE * BOARD_SIZE - NUM_MINES) {
            cout << "Congratulations! You uncovered all cells without detonating any mines." << endl;
            gameWon = true;
        }
    }
    return 0;
}
```

54. Hangman with ASCII Art

```
#include <iostream>
#include <string>
#include <vector>
using namespace std;
void drawHangman(int attempts) {
    if (attempts == 0) {
        cout << "  _________" << endl;
        cout << "  |       |" << endl;
        cout << "  |        " << endl;
        cout << "  |        " << endl;
        cout << "  |        " << endl;
        cout << "  |        " << endl;
        cout << "  |________" << endl;
    } else if (attempts == 1) {
        cout << "  _________" << endl;
        cout << "  |       |" << endl;
        cout << "  |       O" << endl;
        cout << "  |        " << endl;
        cout << "  |        " << endl;
        cout << "  |        " << endl;
        cout << "  |________" << endl;
    } else if (attempts == 2) {
        cout << "  _________" << endl;
        cout << "  |       |" << endl;
        cout << "  |       O" << endl;
        cout << "  |       |" << endl;
        cout << "  |        " << endl;
        cout << "  |        " << endl;
        cout << "  |________" << endl;
    } else if (attempts == 3) {
        cout << "  _________" << endl;
        cout << "  |       |" << endl;
        cout << "  |       O" << endl;
        cout << "  |      /|" << endl;
```

```
        cout << "  |         " << endl;
        cout << "  |         " << endl;
        cout << "  |_________" << endl;
    } else if (attempts == 4) {
        cout << "   _________" << endl;
        cout << "  |        |" << endl;
        cout << "  |        O" << endl;
        cout << "  |       /|\\" << endl;
        cout << "  |         " << endl;
        cout << "  |         " << endl;
        cout << "  |_________" << endl;
    } else if (attempts == 5) {
        cout << "   _________" << endl;
        cout << "  |        |" << endl;
        cout << "  |        O" << endl;
        cout << "  |       /|\\" << endl;
        cout << "  |       / " << endl;
        cout << "  |         " << endl;
        cout << "  |_________" << endl;
    } else {
        cout << "   _________" << endl;
        cout << "  |        |" << endl;
        cout << "  |        O" << endl;
        cout << "  |       /|\\" << endl;
        cout << "  |       / \\" << endl;
        cout << "  |         " << endl;
        cout << "  |_________" << endl;
    }
}
bool contains(const string& word, char letter) {
    for (char c : word) {
        if (c == letter) {
            return true;
        }
```

```
    }
    return false;
}
string getHiddenWord(const string& word, const vector<char>& guessedLetters) {
    string hiddenWord = word;
    for (int i = 0; i < hiddenWord.length(); ++i) {
        if (hiddenWord[i] != ' ' && !contains(guessedLetters, hiddenWord[i])) {
            hiddenWord[i] = '_';
        }
    }
    return hiddenWord;
}
int main() {
    string word = "hangman game";
    vector<char> guessedLetters;
    int attempts = 0;
    cout << "Welcome to Hangman!" << endl;
    while (true) {
        cout << endl;
        drawHangman(attempts);
        cout << "Word: " << getHiddenWord(word, guessedLetters) << endl;
        // Check if the player has won
        if (getHiddenWord(word, guessedLetters) == word) {
            cout << "Congratulations! You've guessed the word correctly: " << word << endl;
            break;
        }
        // Check if the player has lost
        if (attempts == 6) {
            cout << "Sorry, you've run out of attempts. The word was: " << word << endl;
            break;
        }
        cout << "Guess a letter: ";
        char guess;
        cin >> guess;
```

```
        if (contains(word, guess)) {
            guessedLetters.push_back(guess);
            cout << "Correct guess!" << endl;
        } else {
            attempts++;
            cout << "Incorrect guess!" << endl;
        }
    }
    return 0;
}
```

55. Simple Cricket Game

```
#include <iostream>
#include <cstdlib>
#include <ctime>
using namespace std;
// Function to simulate a ball and return the runs scored
int simulateBall() {
    int runs[] = {0, 1, 2, 3, 4, 6, -1}; // -1 represents a wicket
    int randomIndex = rand() % 7;
    return runs[randomIndex];
}
int main() {
    srand(time(0));
    int totalRuns = 0;
    int wickets = 0;
    int balls = 0;
    cout << "Welcome to Simple Cricket Game!" << endl;
    while (wickets < 10) {
        cout << "Press Enter to bowl...";
        cin.ignore(); // Wait for user to press Enter
        int runsScored = simulateBall();
        if (runsScored >= 0) {
            totalRuns += runsScored;
            balls++;
            cout << "Runs scored: " << runsScored << endl;
            cout << "Total Runs: " << totalRuns << " / " << wickets << " in " << balls << " balls" << endl;
        } else {
            wickets++;
            balls++;
            cout << "Out! Total Runs: " << totalRuns << " / " << wickets << " in " << balls << " balls" <<
endl;
            if (wickets == 10) {
                cout << "All out! Game over." << endl;
                break;
            }
```

```
        }
    }
    return 0;
}
```

56. Fruit Ninja-style Game

```
#include <SFML/Graphics.hpp>
#include <vector>
#include <ctime>
#include <cstdlib>
using namespace std;
const int WINDOW_WIDTH = 800;
const int WINDOW_HEIGHT = 600;
const int FRUIT_SIZE = 50;
const int MAX_FRUITS = 5;
const float GRAVITY = 0.2f;
struct Fruit {
    sf::CircleShape shape;
    sf::Vector2f velocity;
};
void updateFruits(vector<Fruit>& fruits) {
    for (auto& fruit : fruits) {
        fruit.shape.move(fruit.velocity);
        fruit.velocity.y += GRAVITY;
    }
}
void drawFruits(sf::RenderWindow& window, const vector<Fruit>& fruits) {
    for (const auto& fruit : fruits) {
        window.draw(fruit.shape);
    }
}
void generateFruit(vector<Fruit>& fruits) {
    if (fruits.size() < MAX_FRUITS) {
        Fruit fruit;
        fruit.shape.setRadius(FRUIT_SIZE / 2);
        fruit.shape.setFillColor(sf::Color::Red);
        fruit.shape.setPosition(rand() % (WINDOW_WIDTH - FRUIT_SIZE), WINDOW_HEIGHT -
FRUIT_SIZE);
        fruit.velocity.x = (rand() % 6) - 3; // Random horizontal velocity
        fruit.velocity.y = -10; // Initial upward velocity
```

```
        fruits.push_back(fruit);
    }
}
int main() {
    srand(time(0));
    sf::RenderWindow window(sf::VideoMode(WINDOW_WIDTH, WINDOW_HEIGHT), "Fruit
Ninja");
    vector<Fruit> fruits;
    sf::Clock clock;
    sf::Time timeSinceLastUpdate = sf::Time::Zero;
    sf::Time TimePerFrame = sf::seconds(1.f / 60.f); // 60 frames per second
    while (window.isOpen()) {
        sf::Event event;
        while (window.pollEvent(event)) {
            if (event.type == sf::Event::Closed)
                window.close();
        }
        sf::Time dt = clock.restart();
        timeSinceLastUpdate += dt;
        while (timeSinceLastUpdate > TimePerFrame) {
            timeSinceLastUpdate -= TimePerFrame;
            updateFruits(fruits);
            // Check for fruit to slice (mouse click)
            if (sf::Mouse::isButtonPressed(sf::Mouse::Left)) {
                sf::Vector2i mousePos = sf::Mouse::getPosition(window);
                for (auto it = fruits.begin(); it != fruits.end();) {
                    if (it->shape.getGlobalBounds().contains(mousePos.x, mousePos.y)) {
                        it = fruits.erase(it); // Slice the fruit
                    } else {
                        ++it;
                    }
                }
            }
            // Generate new fruits
```

```
            generateFruit(fruits);
        }
        window.clear();
        drawFruits(window, fruits);
        window.display();
    }
    return 0;
}
```

57. Ping Pong Game

```
#include <SFML/Graphics.hpp>
// Window dimensions
const int WINDOW_WIDTH = 800;
const int WINDOW_HEIGHT = 600;
// Paddle dimensions
const int PADDLE_WIDTH = 20;
const int PADDLE_HEIGHT = 100;
// Ball dimensions
const int BALL_RADIUS = 10;
// Paddle speed
const float PADDLE_SPEED = 0.6f;
int main() {
    // Create the window
    sf::RenderWindow window(sf::VideoMode(WINDOW_WIDTH, WINDOW_HEIGHT), "Ping
Pong");
    // Create left paddle
    sf::RectangleShape leftPaddle(sf::Vector2f(PADDLE_WIDTH, PADDLE_HEIGHT));
    leftPaddle.setPosition(10, WINDOW_HEIGHT / 2 - PADDLE_HEIGHT / 2);
    leftPaddle.setFillColor(sf::Color::Green);
    // Create right paddle
    sf::RectangleShape rightPaddle(sf::Vector2f(PADDLE_WIDTH, PADDLE_HEIGHT));
    rightPaddle.setPosition(WINDOW_WIDTH - PADDLE_WIDTH - 10, WINDOW_HEIGHT / 2 -
PADDLE_HEIGHT / 2);
    rightPaddle.setFillColor(sf::Color::Blue);
    // Create the ball
    sf::CircleShape ball(BALL_RADIUS);
    ball.setPosition(WINDOW_WIDTH / 2 - BALL_RADIUS / 2, WINDOW_HEIGHT / 2 -
BALL_RADIUS / 2);
    ball.setFillColor(sf::Color::Red);
    float ballVelocityX = -0.3f;
    float ballVelocityY = -0.3f;
    // Main game loop
    while (window.isOpen()) {
        // Handle events
```

```
    sf::Event event;
    while (window.pollEvent(event)) {
      if (event.type == sf::Event::Closed)
        window.close();
    }
    // Move paddles
    if (sf::Keyboard::isKeyPressed(sf::Keyboard::W) && leftPaddle.getPosition().y > 0)
      leftPaddle.move(0, -PADDLE_SPEED);
    if (sf::Keyboard::isKeyPressed(sf::Keyboard::S) && leftPaddle.getPosition().y +
PADDLE_HEIGHT < WINDOW_HEIGHT)
      leftPaddle.move(0, PADDLE_SPEED);
    if (sf::Keyboard::isKeyPressed(sf::Keyboard::Up) && rightPaddle.getPosition().y > 0)
      rightPaddle.move(0, -PADDLE_SPEED);
    if (sf::Keyboard::isKeyPressed(sf::Keyboard::Down) && rightPaddle.getPosition().y +
PADDLE_HEIGHT < WINDOW_HEIGHT)
      rightPaddle.move(0, PADDLE_SPEED);
    // Move the ball
    ball.move(ballVelocityX, ballVelocityY);
    // Collision detection with top and bottom walls
    if (ball.getPosition().y <= 0 || ball.getPosition().y + BALL_RADIUS * 2 >=
WINDOW_HEIGHT)
      ballVelocityY = -ballVelocityY;
    // Collision detection with paddles
    if (ball.getGlobalBounds().intersects(leftPaddle.getGlobalBounds()) ||
      ball.getGlobalBounds().intersects(rightPaddle.getGlobalBounds()))
      ballVelocityX = -ballVelocityX;
    // Reset ball position if it goes out of bounds
    if (ball.getPosition().x <= 0 || ball.getPosition().x + BALL_RADIUS * 2 >= WINDOW_WIDTH)
      ball.setPosition(WINDOW_WIDTH / 2 - BALL_RADIUS / 2, WINDOW_HEIGHT / 2 -
BALL_RADIUS / 2);
    // Clear the window
    window.clear();
    // Draw objects
    window.draw(leftPaddle);
```

```
        window.draw(rightPaddle);
        window.draw(ball);
        // Display the window
        window.display();
    }
    return 0;
}
```

58. Guitar Hero-style Rhythm Game

```
#include <SFML/Graphics.hpp>
#include <vector>
#include <ctime>
#include <cstdlib>
using namespace std;
// Window dimensions
const int WINDOW_WIDTH = 800;
const int WINDOW_HEIGHT = 600;
// Note speed
const float NOTE_SPEED = 0.2f;
// Lane dimensions
const int LANE_WIDTH = 150;
// Note dimensions
const int NOTE_WIDTH = 50;
const int NOTE_HEIGHT = 50;
struct Note {
   sf::RectangleShape shape;
   bool active;
};
void updateNotes(vector<Note>& notes) {
   for (auto& note : notes) {
      if (note.active) {
         note.shape.move(0, NOTE_SPEED);
      }
   }
}
void drawNotes(sf::RenderWindow& window, const vector<Note>& notes) {
   for (const auto& note : notes) {
      if (note.active) {
         window.draw(note.shape);
      }
   }
}
void generateNote(vector<Note>& notes) {
```

```
    Note note;
    note.shape.setSize(sf::Vector2f(NOTE_WIDTH, NOTE_HEIGHT));
    note.shape.setFillColor(sf::Color::Yellow);
    note.shape.setPosition(rand() % (WINDOW_WIDTH - LANE_WIDTH - NOTE_WIDTH), -
NOTE_HEIGHT);
    note.active = true;
    notes.push_back(note);
}
int main() {
    srand(time(0));
    sf::RenderWindow window(sf::VideoMode(WINDOW_WIDTH, WINDOW_HEIGHT), "Rhythm
Game");
    vector<Note> notes;
    sf::Clock clock;
    sf::Time timeSinceLastUpdate = sf::Time::Zero;
    sf::Time TimePerFrame = sf::seconds(1.f / 60.f); // 60 frames per second
    while (window.isOpen()) {
        sf::Event event;
        while (window.pollEvent(event)) {
            if (event.type == sf::Event::Closed)
                window.close();
        }
        sf::Time dt = clock.restart();
        timeSinceLastUpdate += dt;
        while (timeSinceLastUpdate > TimePerFrame) {
            timeSinceLastUpdate -= TimePerFrame;
            updateNotes(notes);
            // Generate new notes
            if (rand() % 100 < 5) {
                generateNote(notes);
            }
        }
        window.clear();
        drawNotes(window, notes);
```

```
        window.display();
    }
    return 0;
}
```

59. Color Matching Game

```
#include <SFML/Graphics.hpp>
#include <iostream>
#include <ctime>
#include <cstdlib>
#include <string>
using namespace std;
const int WINDOW_WIDTH = 800;
const int WINDOW_HEIGHT = 600;
const sf::Color COLORS[] = { sf::Color::Red, sf::Color::Green, sf::Color::Blue, sf::Color::Yellow };
const string COLOR_NAMES[] = { "Red", "Green", "Blue", "Yellow" };
int main() {
    srand(time(0));
    sf::RenderWindow window(sf::VideoMode(WINDOW_WIDTH, WINDOW_HEIGHT), "Color
Matching Game");
    sf::Font font;
    if (!font.loadFromFile("arial.ttf")) {
        cerr << "Font loading failed!" << endl;
        return 1;
    }
    sf::Text colorText("", font, 48);
    colorText.setFillColor(sf::Color::White);
    colorText.setStyle(sf::Text::Bold);
    sf::Text promptText("Type the color of the text:", font, 24);
    promptText.setFillColor(sf::Color::White);
    promptText.setPosition(50, WINDOW_HEIGHT / 2);
    int score = 0;
    while (window.isOpen()) {
        sf::Event event;
        while (window.pollEvent(event)) {
            if (event.type == sf::Event::Closed)
                window.close();
            else if (event.type == sf::Event::TextEntered) {
                if (event.text.unicode >= 32 && event.text.unicode <= 126) {
                    char typedChar = static_cast<char>(event.text.unicode);
```

```
                if (typedChar == '\b') {
                    if (!colorText.getString().isEmpty())
                        colorText.setString(colorText.getString().substring(0, colorText.getString().getSize()
- 1));
                } else {
                    colorText.setString(colorText.getString() + typedChar);
                }
            }
        }
    }
    int colorIndex = rand() % 4;
    int nameIndex = rand() % 4;
    colorText.setString(COLOR_NAMES[nameIndex]);
    colorText.setFillColor(COLORS[colorIndex]);
    window.clear();
    window.draw(promptText);
    window.draw(colorText);
    window.display();
    if (sf::Keyboard::isKeyPressed(sf::Keyboard::Return)) {
        if (colorText.getString().toAnsiString() == COLOR_NAMES[colorIndex]) {
            score++;
            cout << "Correct! Score: " << score << endl;
        } else {
            cout << "Wrong! Score: " << score << endl;
        }
        colorText.setString("");
    }
}    return 0; }
```

60. Simple Chatbot Game

```
#include <iostream>
#include <string>
#include <vector>
using namespace std;
// Function to get user input
string getUserInput() {
    string input;
    cout << "You: ";
    getline(cin, input);
    return input;
}
// Function to simulate chatbot responses
string getChatbotResponse(const string& input) {
    // Simple chatbot responses based on user input
    if (input.find("hello") != string::npos || input.find("hi") != string::npos)
        return "Chatbot: Hello there!";
    else if (input.find("how are you") != string::npos)
        return "Chatbot: I'm doing fine, thank you!";
    else if (input.find("your name") != string::npos)
        return "Chatbot: My name is Chatbot!";
    else if (input.find("age") != string::npos)
        return "Chatbot: I don't have an age!";
    else if (input.find("bye") != string::npos || input.find("goodbye") != string::npos)
        return "Chatbot: Goodbye! Have a great day!";
    else
        return "Chatbot: I'm sorry, I didn't understand.";
}
int main() {
    cout << "Welcome to Chatbot Game!" << endl;
    cout << "Chatbot: Type 'bye' to exit." << endl;
    // Main loop to interact with the chatbot
    while (true) {
        string userInput = getUserInput();
        if (userInput == "bye")
```

```
            break;
        string chatbotResponse = getChatbotResponse(userInput);
        cout << chatbotResponse << endl;
    }
    return 0;
}
```

61. Bouncing Ball Animation

```
#include <SFML/Graphics.hpp>
int main() {
   const int WINDOW_WIDTH = 800;
   const int WINDOW_HEIGHT = 600;
   const int BALL_RADIUS = 30;
   const float BALL_SPEED = 0.2f;
   sf::RenderWindow window(sf::VideoMode(WINDOW_WIDTH, WINDOW_HEIGHT), "Bouncing
Ball Animation");
   sf::CircleShape ball(BALL_RADIUS);
   ball.setFillColor(sf::Color::Red);
   ball.setPosition(WINDOW_WIDTH / 2 - BALL_RADIUS, WINDOW_HEIGHT / 2 -
BALL_RADIUS);
   float ballVelocityX = BALL_SPEED;
   float ballVelocityY = BALL_SPEED;
   while (window.isOpen()) {
      sf::Event event;
      while (window.pollEvent(event)) {
         if (event.type == sf::Event::Closed)
            window.close();
      }
      ball.move(ballVelocityX, ballVelocityY);
      if (ball.getPosition().x <= 0 || ball.getPosition().x + BALL_RADIUS * 2 >= WINDOW_WIDTH)
         ballVelocityX = -ballVelocityX;
      if (ball.getPosition().y <= 0 || ball.getPosition().y + BALL_RADIUS * 2 >=
WINDOW_HEIGHT)
         ballVelocityY = -ballVelocityY;
      window.clear();
      window.draw(ball);
      window.display();
   }    return 0; }
```

62. Doodle Jump-style Game

```
#include <SFML/Graphics.hpp>
#include <vector>
#include <iostream>
// Define constants
const int WINDOW_WIDTH = 800;
const int WINDOW_HEIGHT = 600;
const float GRAVITY = 0.5f;
const float PLATFORM_HEIGHT = 20.0f;
const float PLATFORM_WIDTH = 100.0f;
const float DOODLE_RADIUS = 20.0f;
const float DOODLE_JUMP_VELOCITY = -10.0f;
// Structure for platforms
struct Platform {
   float x, y;
};
// Function to check collision between doodle and platform
bool checkCollision(const sf::CircleShape& doodle, const Platform& platform) {
   float doodleX = doodle.getPosition().x + DOODLE_RADIUS;
   float doodleY = doodle.getPosition().y + DOODLE_RADIUS;
   return doodleX >= platform.x && doodleX <= platform.x + PLATFORM_WIDTH &&
        doodleY >= platform.y && doodleY <= platform.y + PLATFORM_HEIGHT;
}
int main() {
   sf::RenderWindow window(sf::VideoMode(WINDOW_WIDTH, WINDOW_HEIGHT), "Doodle
Jump");
   // Create doodle
   sf::CircleShape doodle(DOODLE_RADIUS);
   doodle.setFillColor(sf::Color::Blue);
   doodle.setPosition(WINDOW_WIDTH / 2 - DOODLE_RADIUS, WINDOW_HEIGHT / 2 -
DOODLE_RADIUS);
   // Create platform
   std::vector<Platform> platforms;
   platforms.push_back({WINDOW_WIDTH / 2 - PLATFORM_WIDTH / 2, WINDOW_HEIGHT -
PLATFORM_HEIGHT});
```

```
    // Main game loop
    while (window.isOpen()) {
        sf::Event event;
        while (window.pollEvent(event)) {
            if (event.type == sf::Event::Closed)
                window.close();
            if (event.type == sf::Event::KeyPressed) {
                if (event.key.code == sf::Keyboard::Space) {
                    doodle.move(0, DOODLE_JUMP_VELOCITY); // Jump when space is pressed
                }
            }
        }
        // Apply gravity to doodle
        doodle.move(0, GRAVITY);
        // Check collision with platforms
        for (const auto& platform : platforms) {
            if (checkCollision(doodle, platform)) {
                // If doodle collides with platform, reset velocity
                doodle.setPosition(doodle.getPosition().x, platform.y - 2 * DOODLE_RADIUS);
                break;
            }
        }
        // If doodle falls below the window, reset its position
        if (doodle.getPosition().y > WINDOW_HEIGHT) {
            doodle.setPosition(WINDOW_WIDTH / 2 - DOODLE_RADIUS, WINDOW_HEIGHT / 2 -
DOODLE_RADIUS);
        }
        // Draw everything
        window.clear();
        window.draw(doodle);
        for (const auto& platform : platforms) {
            sf::RectangleShape platformShape(sf::Vector2f(PLATFORM_WIDTH,
PLATFORM_HEIGHT));
            platformShape.setPosition(platform.x, platform.y);
```

```
            platformShape.setFillColor(sf::Color::Green);
            window.draw(platformShape);
        }
        window.display();
    }
    return 0;
}
```

63. Reaction Time with Sound Effects

```
#include <SFML/Audio.hpp>
#include <SFML/Graphics.hpp>
#include <iostream>
#include <cstdlib>
#include <ctime>
int main() {
  srand(time(0));
  sf::RenderWindow window(sf::VideoMode(400, 200), "Reaction Time Test");
  sf::Font font;
  if (!font.loadFromFile("arial.ttf")) {
    std::cerr << "Font loading failed!" << std::endl;
    return 1;
  }
  sf::Text promptText("Press any key when you see 'Go!'", font, 24);
  promptText.setPosition(50, 50);
  promptText.setFillColor(sf::Color::White);
  sf::Text resultText("", font, 24);
  resultText.setPosition(50, 100);
  sf::SoundBuffer buffer;
  if (!buffer.loadFromFile("beep.wav")) {
    std::cerr << "Sound loading failed!" << std::endl;
    return 1;
  }
  sf::Sound sound;
  sound.setBuffer(buffer);
  sf::Clock clock;
  bool promptShown = false;
  bool keyPressed = false;
  while (window.isOpen()) {
    sf::Event event;
    while (window.pollEvent(event)) {
      if (event.type == sf::Event::Closed)
        window.close();
      if (event.type == sf::Event::KeyPressed && !keyPressed) {
```

```
            float reactionTime = clock.getElapsedTime().asSeconds();
            clock.restart();
            resultText.setString("Your reaction time: " + std::to_string(reactionTime) + " seconds");
            sound.play();
            keyPressed = true;
          }
        }
        window.clear();
        if (!promptShown) {
          window.draw(promptText);
          promptShown = true;
        } else {
          window.draw(resultText);
        }
        window.display();
    }
    return 0;
}
```

64. Puzzle Platformer

```
#include <SFML/Graphics.hpp>
#include <iostream>
const int WINDOW_WIDTH = 800;
const int WINDOW_HEIGHT = 600;
const float GRAVITY = 0.5f;
const float MOVE_SPEED = 0.2f;
const float JUMP_SPEED = -0.7f;
struct Player {
  sf::RectangleShape shape;
  sf::Vector2f velocity;
  bool onGround;
  Player() : shape(sf::Vector2f(50, 50)), velocity(0, 0), onGround(false) {
    shape.setFillColor(sf::Color::Green);
  }
  void update() {
    shape.move(velocity);
    velocity.y += GRAVITY;
  }
  void handleCollision(sf::RectangleShape& platform) {
    sf::FloatRect playerBounds = shape.getGlobalBounds();
    sf::FloatRect platformBounds = platform.getGlobalBounds();
    if (playerBounds.intersects(platformBounds)) {
      float overlapX = std::min(playerBounds.left + playerBounds.width, platformBounds.left +
platformBounds.width) -
              std::max(playerBounds.left, platformBounds.left);
      float overlapY = std::min(playerBounds.top + playerBounds.height, platformBounds.top +
platformBounds.height) -
              std::max(playerBounds.top, platformBounds.top);
      if (overlapX < overlapY) {
        // Colliding from the side
        if (velocity.x > 0)
          shape.move(-overlapX, 0);
        else
          shape.move(overlapX, 0);
```

```
            velocity.x = 0;
        } else {
            // Colliding from above or below
            if (velocity.y > 0) {
                shape.move(0, -overlapY);
                velocity.y = 0;
                onGround = true;
            } else {
                shape.move(0, overlapY);
                velocity.y = 0;
            }
        }
    }
}
void jump() {
    if (onGround) {
        velocity.y = JUMP_SPEED;
        onGround = false;
    }
}

void moveLeft() {
    velocity.x = -MOVE_SPEED;
}
void moveRight() {
    velocity.x = MOVE_SPEED;
}
void stop() {
    velocity.x = 0;
}
};
int main() {
    sf::RenderWindow window(sf::VideoMode(WINDOW_WIDTH, WINDOW_HEIGHT), "Puzzle
Platformer");
```

```
    window.setFramerateLimit(60);
    Player player;
    player.shape.setPosition(50, 50);
    sf::RectangleShape platform(sf::Vector2f(100, 20));
    platform.setFillColor(sf::Color::Red);
    platform.setPosition(200, 300);
    while (window.isOpen()) {
        sf::Event event;
        while (window.pollEvent(event)) {
            if (event.type == sf::Event::Closed)
                window.close();
            if (event.type == sf::Event::KeyPressed) {
                if (event.key.code == sf::Keyboard::Space)
                    player.jump();
                else if (event.key.code == sf::Keyboard::A)
                    player.moveLeft();
                else if (event.key.code == sf::Keyboard::D)
                    player.moveRight();
            }
            if (event.type == sf::Event::KeyReleased) {
                if (event.key.code == sf::Keyboard::A || event.key.code == sf::Keyboard::D)
                    player.stop();
            }
        }
        player.update();
        player.handleCollision(platform);
        window.clear();
        window.draw(player.shape);
        window.draw(platform);
        window.display();
    }
    return 0;
}
```

65. Balloon Pop Game

```
#include <SFML/Graphics.hpp>
#include <cstdlib>
#include <ctime>
const int WINDOW_WIDTH = 800;
const int WINDOW_HEIGHT = 600;
const int BALLOON_RADIUS = 30;
const int MAX_BALLOON_SPEED = 5;
const int MIN_BALLOON_SPEED = 1;
const int POP_DISTANCE = 50;
struct Balloon {
   sf::CircleShape shape;
   sf::Vector2f velocity;
   Balloon(float x, float y) {
      shape.setRadius(BALLOON_RADIUS);
      shape.setFillColor(sf::Color::Red);
      shape.setPosition(x, y);
      velocity.x = rand() % (MAX_BALLOON_SPEED - MIN_BALLOON_SPEED + 1) +
MIN_BALLOON_SPEED;
      velocity.y = rand() % (MAX_BALLOON_SPEED - MIN_BALLOON_SPEED + 1) +
MIN_BALLOON_SPEED;
   }
};
int main() {
   srand(time(0));
   sf::RenderWindow window(sf::VideoMode(WINDOW_WIDTH, WINDOW_HEIGHT), "Balloon
Pop Game");
   std::vector<Balloon> balloons;
   while (window.isOpen()) {
      sf::Event event;
      while (window.pollEvent(event)) {
         if (event.type == sf::Event::Closed)
            window.close();
         if (event.type == sf::Event::MouseButtonPressed) {
            if (event.mouseButton.button == sf::Mouse::Left) {
```

```
                    sf::Vector2i mousePosition = sf::Mouse::getPosition(window);
                    for (auto it = balloons.begin(); it != balloons.end(); ++it) {
                        float dx = mousePosition.x - it->shape.getPosition().x;
                        float dy = mousePosition.y - it->shape.getPosition().y;
                        float distance = sqrt(dx * dx + dy * dy);
                        if (distance <= BALLOON_RADIUS + POP_DISTANCE) {
                            balloons.erase(it);
                            break;
                        }
                    }
                }
            }
        }
        if (rand() % 100 < 5) {
            float x = rand() % (WINDOW_WIDTH - 2 * BALLOON_RADIUS) + BALLOON_RADIUS;
            float y = WINDOW_HEIGHT;
            balloons.push_back(Balloon(x, y));
        }
        window.clear();
        for (auto& balloon : balloons) {
            balloon.shape.move(balloon.velocity);
            window.draw(balloon.shape);
        }
        window.display();
    }
    return 0;
}
```

66. Platformer with Double Jump

```
#include <SFML/Graphics.hpp>
#include <iostream>
const int WINDOW_WIDTH = 800;
const int WINDOW_HEIGHT = 600;
const float GRAVITY = 0.5f;
const float MOVE_SPEED = 0.2f;
const float JUMP_SPEED = -0.7f;
const int MAX_JUMPS = 2;
struct Player {
    sf::RectangleShape shape;
    sf::Vector2f velocity;
    int jumpsLeft;
    Player() : shape(sf::Vector2f(50, 50)), velocity(0, 0), jumpsLeft(MAX_JUMPS) {
        shape.setFillColor(sf::Color::Green);
    }
    void update() {
        shape.move(velocity);
        velocity.y += GRAVITY;
    }
    void jump() {
        if (jumpsLeft > 0) {
            velocity.y = JUMP_SPEED;
            jumpsLeft--;
        }
    }
    void moveLeft() {
        velocity.x = -MOVE_SPEED;
    }
    void moveRight() {
        velocity.x = MOVE_SPEED;
    }
    void stop() {
        velocity.x = 0;
    }
```

```
    void resetJumps() {
        jumpsLeft = MAX_JUMPS;
    }
};
int main() {
    sf::RenderWindow window(sf::VideoMode(WINDOW_WIDTH, WINDOW_HEIGHT),
"Platformer with Double Jump");
    window.setFramerateLimit(60);
    Player player;
    player.shape.setPosition(50, 50);
    bool isJumping = false;
    while (window.isOpen()) {
        sf::Event event;
        while (window.pollEvent(event)) {
            if (event.type == sf::Event::Closed)
                window.close();
            if (event.type == sf::Event::KeyPressed) {
                if (event.key.code == sf::Keyboard::Space && (player.jumpsLeft > 0 || isJumping)) {
                    player.jump();
                    isJumping = true;
                } else if (event.key.code == sf::Keyboard::A)
                    player.moveLeft();
                else if (event.key.code == sf::Keyboard::D)
                    player.moveRight();
            }
            if (event.type == sf::Event::KeyReleased) {
                if (event.key.code == sf::Keyboard::A || event.key.code == sf::Keyboard::D)
                    player.stop();
                if (event.key.code == sf::Keyboard::Space)
                    isJumping = false;
            }
        }
        player.update();
        if (player.shape.getPosition().y > WINDOW_HEIGHT) {
```

```
            player.shape.setPosition(50, 50);
            player.resetJumps();
        }
        window.clear();
        window.draw(player.shape);
        window.display();
    }
    return 0;
}
```

67. Galaga-style Shooter Game

```
#include <SFML/Graphics.hpp>
#include <iostream>
#include <vector>
const int WINDOW_WIDTH = 800;
const int WINDOW_HEIGHT = 600;
const int PLAYER_SIZE = 50;
const int ENEMY_SIZE = 30;
const float PLAYER_SPEED = 5.0f;
const float ENEMY_SPEED = 3.0f;
const int MAX_ENEMIES = 5;
struct Player {
  sf::RectangleShape shape;
  int health;
  Player() : shape(sf::Vector2f(PLAYER_SIZE, PLAYER_SIZE)), health(100) {
    shape.setFillColor(sf::Color::Blue);
    shape.setPosition(WINDOW_WIDTH / 2 - PLAYER_SIZE / 2, WINDOW_HEIGHT -
PLAYER_SIZE * 2);
  }
  void moveLeft() {
    if (shape.getPosition().x > 0)
      shape.move(-PLAYER_SPEED, 0);
  }
  void moveRight() {
    if (shape.getPosition().x < WINDOW_WIDTH - PLAYER_SIZE)
      shape.move(PLAYER_SPEED, 0);
  }
  void moveUp() {
    if (shape.getPosition().y > 0)
      shape.move(0, -PLAYER_SPEED);
  }
```

```
    void moveDown() {
        if (shape.getPosition().y < WINDOW_HEIGHT - PLAYER_SIZE)
            shape.move(0, PLAYER_SPEED);
    }
};
struct Enemy {
    sf::RectangleShape shape;
    bool alive;
    Enemy(float x, float y) : shape(sf::Vector2f(ENEMY_SIZE, ENEMY_SIZE)), alive(true) {
        shape.setFillColor(sf::Color::Red);
        shape.setPosition(x, y);
    }
    void move() {
        shape.move(0, ENEMY_SPEED);
    }
};
int main() {
    sf::RenderWindow window(sf::VideoMode(WINDOW_WIDTH, WINDOW_HEIGHT), "Galaga-
style Shooter Game");
    window.setFramerateLimit(60);
    Player player;
    std::vector<Enemy> enemies;
    while (window.isOpen()) {
        sf::Event event;
        while (window.pollEvent(event)) {
            if (event.type == sf::Event::Closed)
                window.close();
            if (event.type == sf::Event::KeyPressed) {
                if (event.key.code == sf::Keyboard::A)
                    player.moveLeft();
                else if (event.key.code == sf::Keyboard::D)
                    player.moveRight();
                else if (event.key.code == sf::Keyboard::W)
                    player.moveUp();
                else if (event.key.code == sf::Keyboard::S)
```

```
                player.moveDown();
            }
        }
        if (enemies.size() < MAX_ENEMIES) {
            float x = rand() % (WINDOW_WIDTH - ENEMY_SIZE);
            enemies.push_back(Enemy(x, -ENEMY_SIZE));
        }
        for (auto& enemy : enemies) {
            if (enemy.shape.getPosition().y > WINDOW_HEIGHT)
                enemy.alive = false;
            if (enemy.alive)
                enemy.move();
        }
        enemies.erase(std::remove_if(enemies.begin(), enemies.end(), [](const Enemy& enemy) { return
!enemy.alive; }), enemies.end());
        window.clear();
        window.draw(player.shape);
        for (const auto& enemy : enemies)
            window.draw(enemy.shape);
        window.display();
    }
    return 0;
}
```

68. Card Sorting Game

```
#include <SFML/Graphics.hpp>
#include <iostream>
#include <vector>
const int WINDOW_WIDTH = 800;
const int WINDOW_HEIGHT = 600;
const int PLAYER_SIZE = 50;
const int ENEMY_SIZE = 30;
const float PLAYER_SPEED = 5.0f;
const float ENEMY_SPEED = 3.0f;
const int MAX_ENEMIES = 5;
struct Player {
    sf::RectangleShape shape;
    int health;
    Player() : shape(sf::Vector2f(PLAYER_SIZE, PLAYER_SIZE)), health(100) {
        shape.setFillColor(sf::Color::Blue);
        shape.setPosition(WINDOW_WIDTH / 2 - PLAYER_SIZE / 2, WINDOW_HEIGHT -
PLAYER_SIZE * 2);
    }
    void moveLeft() {
        if (shape.getPosition().x > 0)
            shape.move(-PLAYER_SPEED, 0);
    }
    void moveRight() {
        if (shape.getPosition().x < WINDOW_WIDTH - PLAYER_SIZE)
            shape.move(PLAYER_SPEED, 0);
    }
    void moveUp() {
        if (shape.getPosition().y > 0)
            shape.move(0, -PLAYER_SPEED);
    }

    void moveDown() {
        if (shape.getPosition().y < WINDOW_HEIGHT - PLAYER_SIZE)
            shape.move(0, PLAYER_SPEED);
```

```
    }
};
struct Enemy {
    sf::RectangleShape shape;
    bool alive;
    Enemy(float x, float y) : shape(sf::Vector2f(ENEMY_SIZE, ENEMY_SIZE)), alive(true) {
        shape.setFillColor(sf::Color::Red);
        shape.setPosition(x, y);
    }
    void move() {
        shape.move(0, ENEMY_SPEED);
    }
};
int main() {
    sf::RenderWindow window(sf::VideoMode(WINDOW_WIDTH, WINDOW_HEIGHT), "Galaga-
style Shooter Game");
    window.setFramerateLimit(60);
    Player player;
    std::vector<Enemy> enemies;
    while (window.isOpen()) {
        sf::Event event;
        while (window.pollEvent(event)) {
            if (event.type == sf::Event::Closed)
                window.close();
            if (event.type == sf::Event::KeyPressed) {
                if (event.key.code == sf::Keyboard::A)
                    player.moveLeft();
                else if (event.key.code == sf::Keyboard::D)
                    player.moveRight();
                else if (event.key.code == sf::Keyboard::W)
                    player.moveUp();
                else if (event.key.code == sf::Keyboard::S)
                    player.moveDown();
            }
```

```
        }
        if (enemies.size() < MAX_ENEMIES) {
            float x = rand() % (WINDOW_WIDTH - ENEMY_SIZE);
            enemies.push_back(Enemy(x, -ENEMY_SIZE));
        }
        for (auto& enemy : enemies) {
            if (enemy.shape.getPosition().y > WINDOW_HEIGHT)
                enemy.alive = false;
            if (enemy.alive)
                enemy.move();
        }
        enemies.erase(std::remove_if(enemies.begin(), enemies.end(), [](const Enemy& enemy) { return
!enemy.alive; }), enemies.end());
        window.clear();
        window.draw(player.shape);
        for (const auto& enemy : enemies)
            window.draw(enemy.shape);
        window.display();
    }
    return 0;
}
```

69. Simple Soccer Game

```
#include <SFML/Graphics.hpp>
#include <iostream>
const int WINDOW_WIDTH = 800;
const int WINDOW_HEIGHT = 600;
const float PLAYER_SIZE = 50.0f;
const float BALL_SIZE = 20.0f;
const float PLAYER_SPEED = 5.0f;
const float BALL_SPEED = 5.0f;
struct Player {
   sf::RectangleShape shape;
   sf::Vector2f velocity;
   Player(float x, float y, sf::Color color) {
      shape.setSize(sf::Vector2f(PLAYER_SIZE, PLAYER_SIZE));
      shape.setFillColor(color);
      shape.setPosition(x, y);
   }
   void move(float offsetX, float offsetY) {
      shape.move(offsetX, offsetY);
   }
};
struct Ball {
   sf::CircleShape shape;
   sf::Vector2f velocity;
   Ball(float x, float y) {
      shape.setRadius(BALL_SIZE);
      shape.setFillColor(sf::Color::White);
      shape.setPosition(x, y);
   }
   void move() {
      shape.move(velocity);
   }
};
int main() {
   sf::RenderWindow window(sf::VideoMode(WINDOW_WIDTH, WINDOW_HEIGHT), "Simple
```

```
Soccer Game");
    window.setFramerateLimit(60);
    Player player1(50, WINDOW_HEIGHT / 2 - PLAYER_SIZE / 2, sf::Color::Blue);
    Player player2(WINDOW_WIDTH - 50 - PLAYER_SIZE, WINDOW_HEIGHT / 2 -
PLAYER_SIZE / 2, sf::Color::Red);
    Ball ball(WINDOW_WIDTH / 2 - BALL_SIZE / 2, WINDOW_HEIGHT / 2 - BALL_SIZE / 2);
    while (window.isOpen()) {
        sf::Event event;
        while (window.pollEvent(event)) {
            if (event.type == sf::Event::Closed)
                window.close();
        }
        // Player 1 controls
        if (sf::Keyboard::isKeyPressed(sf::Keyboard::W))
            player1.move(0, -PLAYER_SPEED);
        if (sf::Keyboard::isKeyPressed(sf::Keyboard::S))
            player1.move(0, PLAYER_SPEED);
        // Player 2 controls
        if (sf::Keyboard::isKeyPressed(sf::Keyboard::Up))
            player2.move(0, -PLAYER_SPEED);
        if (sf::Keyboard::isKeyPressed(sf::Keyboard::Down))
            player2.move(0, PLAYER_SPEED);
        // Ball movement
        ball.move();
        // Ball collision with top and bottom walls
        if (ball.shape.getPosition().y <= 0 || ball.shape.getPosition().y >= WINDOW_HEIGHT -
BALL_SIZE) {
            ball.velocity.y = -ball.velocity.y;
        }
        // Ball collision with players
        if (ball.shape.getGlobalBounds().intersects(player1.shape.getGlobalBounds()) ||
            ball.shape.getGlobalBounds().intersects(player2.shape.getGlobalBounds())) {
            ball.velocity.x = -ball.velocity.x;
        }
```

```
        // Ball collision with left and right walls (goal)
        if (ball.shape.getPosition().x <= 0 || ball.shape.getPosition().x >= WINDOW_WIDTH -
BALL_SIZE) {
            ball.shape.setPosition(WINDOW_WIDTH / 2 - BALL_SIZE / 2, WINDOW_HEIGHT / 2 -
BALL_SIZE / 2);
        }
        window.clear(sf::Color::Black);
        window.draw(player1.shape);
        window.draw(player2.shape);
        window.draw(ball.shape);
        window.display();
    }
    return 0;
}
```

70. Archery Shooting Game

```
#include <SFML/Graphics.hpp>
#include <cmath>
#include <iostream>
const int WINDOW_WIDTH = 800;
const int WINDOW_HEIGHT = 600;
const float TARGET_SIZE = 50.0f;
const float ARROW_SIZE = 20.0f;
const float ARROW_SPEED = 10.0f;
struct Arrow {
    sf::RectangleShape shape;
    sf::Vector2f velocity;
    Arrow(float x, float y, float angle) {
        shape.setSize(sf::Vector2f(ARROW_SIZE, 5.0f));
        shape.setFillColor(sf::Color::Black);
        shape.setPosition(x, y);
        shape.setRotation(angle);
        velocity.x = ARROW_SPEED * std::cos(angle * (3.14159 / 180));
        velocity.y = ARROW_SPEED * std::sin(angle * (3.14159 / 180));
    }
    void move() {
        shape.move(velocity);
    }
};
struct Target {
    sf::CircleShape shape;
    Target(float x, float y) {
        shape.setRadius(TARGET_SIZE);
        shape.setFillColor(sf::Color::Red);
        shape.setPosition(x, y);
    }
};
int main() {
    sf::RenderWindow window(sf::VideoMode(WINDOW_WIDTH, WINDOW_HEIGHT), "Archery
Shooting Game");
```

```
    window.setFramerateLimit(60);
    std::vector<Target> targets;
    sf::RectangleShape bow(sf::Vector2f(50, 5));
    bow.setFillColor(sf::Color::Black);
    bow.setPosition(WINDOW_WIDTH / 2 - 25, WINDOW_HEIGHT - 50);
    sf::Vector2f bowOrigin(25, 2.5);
    float bowAngle = 0.0f;
    std::vector<Arrow> arrows;
    while (window.isOpen()) {
        sf::Event event;
        while (window.pollEvent(event)) {
            if (event.type == sf::Event::Closed)
                window.close();
            if (event.type == sf::Event::MouseButtonPressed && event.mouseButton.button ==
sf::Mouse::Left) {
                float mouseX = event.mouseButton.x;
                float mouseY = event.mouseButton.y;
                float dx = mouseX - (bow.getPosition().x + bowOrigin.x);
                float dy = mouseY - (bow.getPosition().y + bowOrigin.y);
                float angle = std::atan2(dy, dx) * (180 / 3.14159);
                arrows.push_back(Arrow(bow.getPosition().x + bowOrigin.x, bow.getPosition().y +
bowOrigin.y, angle));
            }
        }
        // Move arrows
        for (auto& arrow : arrows)
            arrow.move();
        // Remove arrows that are out of bounds
        arrows.erase(std::remove_if(arrows.begin(), arrows.end(), [&](const Arrow& arrow) {
            return arrow.shape.getPosition().x < 0 || arrow.shape.getPosition().x > WINDOW_WIDTH ||
                arrow.shape.getPosition().y < 0 || arrow.shape.getPosition().y > WINDOW_HEIGHT;
        }), arrows.end());
        window.clear(sf::Color::White);
        // Draw targets
```

```
        for (const auto& target : targets)
            window.draw(target.shape);
        // Draw arrows
        for (const auto& arrow : arrows)
            window.draw(arrow.shape);
        // Draw bow
        bow.setRotation(bowAngle);
        window.draw(bow);
        window.display();
    }
    return 0;
}
```

71. Chess Timer

```
#include <SFML/Graphics.hpp>
#include <iostream>
const int WINDOW_WIDTH = 800;
const int WINDOW_HEIGHT = 600;
const float TIMER_START = 60.0f;
int main() {
  sf::RenderWindow window(sf::VideoMode(WINDOW_WIDTH, WINDOW_HEIGHT), "Chess
Timer");
  window.setFramerateLimit(60);
  sf::Font font;
  if (!font.loadFromFile("arial.ttf")) {
    std::cerr << "Font loading failed!" << std::endl;
    return 1;
  }
  sf::Text player1Text;
  player1Text.setFont(font);
  player1Text.setCharacterSize(24);
  player1Text.setFillColor(sf::Color::White);
  player1Text.setPosition(50, 50);
  sf::Text player2Text;
  player2Text.setFont(font);
  player2Text.setCharacterSize(24);
  player2Text.setFillColor(sf::Color::White);
  player2Text.setPosition(50, 100);
  sf::Clock clock;
  float player1Time = TIMER_START;
  float player2Time = TIMER_START;
  bool player1Turn = true;
  while (window.isOpen()) {
    sf::Event event;
    while (window.pollEvent(event)) {
      if (event.type == sf::Event::Closed)
        window.close();
      if (event.type == sf::Event::KeyPressed) {
```

```
            if (event.key.code == sf::Keyboard::Space) {
                if (player1Turn && player1Time > 0)
                    player1Time -= clock.restart().asSeconds();
                else if (!player1Turn && player2Time > 0)
                    player2Time -= clock.restart().asSeconds();
                player1Turn = !player1Turn;
            }
        }
    }
    player1Text.setString("Player 1: " + std::to_string(static_cast<int>(player1Time)) + " sec");
    player2Text.setString("Player 2: " + std::to_string(static_cast<int>(player2Time)) + " sec");
    window.clear(sf::Color::Black);
    window.draw(player1Text);
    window.draw(player2Text);
    window.display();
  }
  return 0;
}
```

72. Emoji Memory Match Game

```
#include <SFML/Graphics.hpp>
#include <iostream>
#include <vector>
#include <algorithm>
#include <random>
const int WINDOW_WIDTH = 800;
const int WINDOW_HEIGHT = 600;
const int CARD_SIZE = 100;
const int NUM_CARDS = 16;
const std::string emojis[] = {"□", "□", "□", "□", "□", "□", "□", "□", "□", "□", "□", "□", "□", "□",
"□", "□"};
struct Card {
    sf::RectangleShape shape;
    sf::Text text;
    std::string emoji;
    bool flipped;
    Card(float x, float y, std::string emoji, sf::Font& font) : emoji(emoji), flipped(false) {
        shape.setSize(sf::Vector2f(CARD_SIZE, CARD_SIZE));
        shape.setFillColor(sf::Color::White);
        shape.setOutlineColor(sf::Color::Black);
        shape.setOutlineThickness(2);
        shape.setPosition(x, y);
        text.setFont(font);
        text.setString("");
        text.setCharacterSize(50);
        text.setFillColor(sf::Color::Black);
        text.setPosition(x + 20, y + 10);
    }
    void flip() {
        flipped = !flipped;
    }
    void draw(sf::RenderWindow& window) {
        if (flipped) {
            text.setString(emoji);
```

```
            window.draw(text);
        } else {
            text.setString("");
            window.draw(shape);
        }
    }
};
int main() {
    sf::RenderWindow window(sf::VideoMode(WINDOW_WIDTH, WINDOW_HEIGHT), "Emoji
Memory Match Game");
    window.setFramerateLimit(60);
    sf::Font font;
    if (!font.loadFromFile("arial.ttf")) {
        std::cerr << "Font loading failed!" << std::endl;
        return 1;
    }
    std::vector<std::string> emojisPool(emojis, emojis + sizeof(emojis) / sizeof(emojis[0]));
    std::vector<Card> cards;
    // Create pairs of cards with emojis
    for (int i = 0; i < NUM_CARDS / 2; ++i) {
        std::random_device rd;
        std::mt19937 rng(rd());
        std::uniform_int_distribution<int> uni(0, emojisPool.size() - 1);
        int randomIndex = uni(rng);
        std::string emoji = emojisPool[randomIndex];
        emojisPool.erase(emojisPool.begin() + randomIndex);
        cards.push_back(Card(i * (CARD_SIZE + 10) + 50, 50, emoji, font));
        cards.push_back(Card(i * (CARD_SIZE + 10) + 50, 200, emoji, font));
    }
    // Shuffle cards
    std::random_shuffle(cards.begin(), cards.end());
    Card* firstCard = nullptr;
    Card* secondCard = nullptr;
    while (window.isOpen()) {
```

```
    sf::Event event;
    while (window.pollEvent(event)) {
      if (event.type == sf::Event::Closed)
        window.close();
      else if (event.type == sf::Event::MouseButtonPressed) {
        if (event.mouseButton.button == sf::Mouse::Left) {
          for (auto& card : cards) {
            if (!card.flipped && card.shape.getGlobalBounds().contains(event.mouseButton.x,
event.mouseButton.y)) {
              card.flip();
              if (!firstCard)
                firstCard = &card;
              else {
                secondCard = &card;
                if (firstCard->emoji != secondCard->emoji) {
                  // Delay flipping back
                  sf::sleep(sf::milliseconds(1000));
                  firstCard->flip();
                  secondCard->flip();
                }
                firstCard = nullptr;
                secondCard = nullptr;
              }
              break;
            }
          }
        }
      }
    }
    window.clear(sf::Color::White);
    for (const auto& card : cards)
      card.draw(window);
    window.display();
  }   return 0; }
```

73. Space Shooter Game

```
#include <SFML/Graphics.hpp>
#include <iostream>
#include <vector>
#include <ctime>
const int WINDOW_WIDTH = 800;
const int WINDOW_HEIGHT = 600;
const float PLAYER_SIZE = 50.0f;
const float ENEMY_SIZE = 30.0f;
const float BULLET_SIZE = 5.0f;
const float PLAYER_SPEED = 5.0f;
const float ENEMY_SPEED = 3.0f;
const float BULLET_SPEED = 7.0f;
const int MAX_ENEMIES = 5;
struct Player {
  sf::RectangleShape shape;
  int health;
  Player() : health(100) {
    shape.setSize(sf::Vector2f(PLAYER_SIZE, PLAYER_SIZE));
    shape.setFillColor(sf::Color::Blue);
    shape.setPosition(WINDOW_WIDTH / 2 - PLAYER_SIZE / 2, WINDOW_HEIGHT -
PLAYER_SIZE * 2);
  }
  void moveLeft() {
    if (shape.getPosition().x > 0)
      shape.move(-PLAYER_SPEED, 0);
  }
  void moveRight() {
    if (shape.getPosition().x < WINDOW_WIDTH - PLAYER_SIZE)
      shape.move(PLAYER_SPEED, 0);
  }
  void moveUp() {
    if (shape.getPosition().y > 0)
      shape.move(0, -PLAYER_SPEED);
  }
```

```
    void moveDown() {
        if (shape.getPosition().y < WINDOW_HEIGHT - PLAYER_SIZE)
            shape.move(0, PLAYER_SPEED);
    }
};
struct Enemy {
    sf::RectangleShape shape;
    bool alive;
    Enemy(float x, float y) : alive(true) {
        shape.setSize(sf::Vector2f(ENEMY_SIZE, ENEMY_SIZE));
        shape.setFillColor(sf::Color::Red);
        shape.setPosition(x, y);
    }
    void move() {
        shape.move(0, ENEMY_SPEED);
    }
};
struct Bullet {
    sf::RectangleShape shape;
    bool alive;
    Bullet(float x, float y) : alive(true) {
        shape.setSize(sf::Vector2f(BULLET_SIZE, BULLET_SIZE));
        shape.setFillColor(sf::Color::Yellow);
        shape.setPosition(x, y);
    }
    void move() {
        shape.move(0, -BULLET_SPEED);
    }
};

int main() {
    sf::RenderWindow window(sf::VideoMode(WINDOW_WIDTH, WINDOW_HEIGHT), "Space
Shooter Game");
    window.setFramerateLimit(60);
```

```
    Player player;
    std::vector<Enemy> enemies;
    std::vector<Bullet> bullets;
    while (window.isOpen()) {
        sf::Event event;
        while (window.pollEvent(event)) {
            if (event.type == sf::Event::Closed)
                window.close();
            if (event.type == sf::Event::KeyPressed) {
                if (event.key.code == sf::Keyboard::A)
                    player.moveLeft();
                else if (event.key.code == sf::Keyboard::D)
                    player.moveRight();
                else if (event.key.code == sf::Keyboard::W)
                    player.moveUp();
                else if (event.key.code == sf::Keyboard::S)
                    player.moveDown();
                else if (event.key.code == sf::Keyboard::Space)
                    bullets.push_back(Bullet(player.shape.getPosition().x + PLAYER_SIZE / 2 -
BULLET_SIZE / 2, player.shape.getPosition().y));
            }
        }
        if (enemies.size() < MAX_ENEMIES) {
            float x = rand() % (WINDOW_WIDTH - ENEMY_SIZE);
            enemies.push_back(Enemy(x, -ENEMY_SIZE));
        }

        for (auto& enemy : enemies) {
            if (enemy.shape.getPosition().y > WINDOW_HEIGHT)
                enemy.alive = false;
            if (enemy.alive)
                enemy.move();
        }
        enemies.erase(std::remove_if(enemies.begin(), enemies.end(), [](const Enemy& enemy) { return
```

```
!enemy.alive; }), enemies.end());
        for (auto& bullet : bullets) {
            if (bullet.shape.getPosition().y < 0)
                bullet.alive = false;
            if (bullet.alive)
                bullet.move();
        }
        bullets.erase(std::remove_if(bullets.begin(), bullets.end(), [](const Bullet& bullet) { return
!bullet.alive; }), bullets.end());
        // Collision detection
        for (auto& bullet : bullets) {
            for (auto& enemy : enemies) {
                if (bullet.shape.getGlobalBounds().intersects(enemy.shape.getGlobalBounds())) {
                    bullet.alive = false;
                    enemy.alive = false;
                }
            }
        }
        window.clear(sf::Color::Black);
        window.draw(player.shape);
        for (const auto& enemy : enemies)
            window.draw(enemy.shape);
        for (const auto& bullet : bullets)
            window.draw(bullet.shape);

        window.display();
    }
    return 0;
}
```

74. Sokoban Puzzle Game

```
#include <SFML/Graphics.hpp>
#include <iostream>
#include <vector>
#include <fstream>
const int TILE_SIZE = 50;
const int NUM_ROWS = 10;
const int NUM_COLS = 10;
struct Tile {
    sf::RectangleShape shape;
    bool isWall;
    bool isBox;
    bool isGoal;
    Tile(bool wall = false, bool box = false, bool goal = false) : isWall(wall), isBox(box), isGoal(goal) {
        shape.setSize(sf::Vector2f(TILE_SIZE, TILE_SIZE));
        shape.setOutlineColor(sf::Color::Black);
        shape.setOutlineThickness(1);
        if (isWall)
            shape.setFillColor(sf::Color::Black);
        else if (isGoal)
            shape.setFillColor(sf::Color::Green);
        else
            shape.setFillColor(sf::Color::White);
    }
    void setPosition(float x, float y) {
        shape.setPosition(x, y);
    }
};
class SokobanGame {
private:
    sf::RenderWindow window;
    std::vector<std::vector<Tile>> tiles;
    sf::Texture playerTexture;
    sf::Sprite playerSprite;
    int playerRow;
```

```
    int playerCol;
public:
    SokobanGame() : window(sf::VideoMode(NUM_COLS * TILE_SIZE, NUM_ROWS *
TILE_SIZE), "Sokoban Puzzle Game") {
        loadLevel("level.txt");
        if (!playerTexture.loadFromFile("player.png")) {
            std::cerr << "Failed to load player texture!" << std::endl;
            return;
        }
        playerSprite.setTexture(playerTexture);
        playerRow = 1;
        playerCol = 1;
        playerSprite.setPosition(playerCol * TILE_SIZE, playerRow * TILE_SIZE);
    }
    void loadLevel(const std::string& filename) {
        std::ifstream file(filename);
        if (!file.is_open()) {
            std::cerr << "Failed to open level file!" << std::endl;
            return;
        }
        tiles.resize(NUM_ROWS);
        for (int i = 0; i < NUM_ROWS; ++i) {
            tiles[i].resize(NUM_COLS);
            for (int j = 0; j < NUM_COLS; ++j) {
                char c;
                file >> c;
                bool isWall = (c == '#');
                bool isBox = (c == 'B');
                bool isGoal = (c == 'G');
                tiles[i][j] = Tile(isWall, isBox, isGoal);
                tiles[i][j].setPosition(j * TILE_SIZE, i * TILE_SIZE);
            }
        }
        file.close();
```

```
    }
    void run() {
        while (window.isOpen()) {
            sf::Event event;
            while (window.pollEvent(event)) {
                if (event.type == sf::Event::Closed)
                    window.close();
                if (event.type == sf::Event::KeyPressed) {
                    if (event.key.code == sf::Keyboard::Up)
                        movePlayer(-1, 0);
                    else if (event.key.code == sf::Keyboard::Down)
                        movePlayer(1, 0);
                    else if (event.key.code == sf::Keyboard::Left)
                        movePlayer(0, -1);
                    else if (event.key.code == sf::Keyboard::Right)
                        movePlayer(0, 1);
                }
            }
            window.clear(sf::Color::White);
            drawTiles();
            window.draw(playerSprite);
            window.display();
        }
    }
    void movePlayer(int dRow, int dCol) {
        int newRow = playerRow + dRow;
        int newCol = playerCol + dCol;
        if (isValidMove(newRow, newCol)) {
            playerRow = newRow;
            playerCol = newCol;
            playerSprite.setPosition(playerCol * TILE_SIZE, playerRow * TILE_SIZE);
        }
    }
    bool isValidMove(int row, int col) {
```

```
        if (row < 0 || row >= NUM_ROWS || col < 0 || col >= NUM_COLS)
            return false;
        if (tiles[row][col].isWall)
            return false;
        if (tiles[row][col].isBox) {
            int newRow = row + (row - playerRow);
            int newCol = col + (col - playerCol);
            if (newRow < 0 || newRow >= NUM_ROWS || newCol < 0 || newCol >= NUM_COLS)
                return false;
            if (tiles[newRow][newCol].isWall || tiles[newRow][newCol].isBox)
                return false;
            tiles[row][col].isBox = false;
            tiles[newRow][newCol].isBox = true;
        }
        return true;
    }
    void drawTiles() {
        for (int i = 0; i < NUM_ROWS; ++i) {
            for (int j = 0; j < NUM_COLS; ++j) {
                window.draw(tiles[i][j].shape);
            }
        }
    }
};
int main() {
    SokobanGame game;
    game.run();
    return 0;
}
```

75. Jungle Adventure Game

```
#include <SFML/Graphics.hpp>

#include <iostream>

const int WINDOW_WIDTH = 800;

const int WINDOW_HEIGHT = 600;

const float PLAYER_SIZE = 50.0f;

const float PLAYER_SPEED = 5.0f;

struct Player {

    sf::RectangleShape shape;

    Player() {

        shape.setSize(sf::Vector2f(PLAYER_SIZE, PLAYER_SIZE));

        shape.setFillColor(sf::Color::Green);

        shape.setPosition(WINDOW_WIDTH / 2 - PLAYER_SIZE / 2, WINDOW_HEIGHT / 2 -
PLAYER_SIZE / 2);

    }

    void move(float offsetX, float offsetY) {

        shape.move(offsetX * PLAYER_SPEED, offsetY * PLAYER_SPEED);

    }

};

int main() {

    sf::RenderWindow window(sf::VideoMode(WINDOW_WIDTH, WINDOW_HEIGHT), "Jungle
Adventure Game");

    window.setFramerateLimit(60);

    Player player;

    while (window.isOpen()) {

        sf::Event event;

        while (window.pollEvent(event)) {

            if (event.type == sf::Event::Closed)

                window.close();
```

```
            if (event.type == sf::Event::KeyPressed) {
                if (event.key.code == sf::Keyboard::W)
                    player.move(0, -1);
                else if (event.key.code == sf::Keyboard::S)
                    player.move(0, 1);
                else if (event.key.code == sf::Keyboard::A)
                    player.move(-1, 0);
                else if (event.key.code == sf::Keyboard::D)
                    player.move(1, 0);
            }
        }
        window.clear(sf::Color::Black);
        window.draw(player.shape);
        window.display();
    }
    return 0;
}
```

www.ingramcontent.com/pod-product-compliance
Lightning Source LLC
Chambersburg PA
CBHW040743170726
48282CB00023B/123
9789334040524